Best of Bridge

5-Ingredient Cooking

125 Recipes for Fast & Easy Meals

Robert
ROSE

For complete cataloguing information, see page 211.

Disclaimer
The recipes in this book have been carefully tested by our kitchen and our tasters. To the best of our knowledge, they are safe and nutritious for ordinary use and users. For those people with food or other allergies, or who have special food requirements or health issues, please read the suggested contents of each recipe carefully and determine whether or not they may create a problem for you. All recipes are used at the risk of the consumer.

We cannot be responsible for any hazards, loss or damage that may occur as a result of any recipe use.

For those with special needs, allergies, requirements or health problems, in the event of any doubt, please contact your medical adviser prior to the use of any recipe.

Design and production: Kevin Cockburn/PageWave Graphics Inc.
Editor: Kathleen Fraser
Indexer: Gillian Watts
Photography and Styling: Ashley Lima

Cover image: Jerk Chicken and Sweet Potato Sheet-Pan Supper (page 108)

The publisher gratefully acknowledges the financial support of our publishing program by the Government of Canada through the Canada Book Fund.

Canada

Published by Robert Rose Inc.
120 Eglinton Avenue East, Suite 800, Toronto, Ontario, Canada M4P 1E2
Tel: (416) 322-6552 Fax: (416) 322-6936
www.robertrose.ca

Printed and bound in China

1 2 3 4 5 6 7 8 9 LEO 28 27 26 25 24 23 22 21 20

*THE KITCHEN IS SEASONED WITH LOVE
AND MAYBE SOME CRUMBS TOO.*

MY COOKING IS FABULOUS — EVEN
THE SMOKE ALARM IS CHEERING ME ON.

CONTENTS

INTRODUCTION

SIMPLICITY IS A FORM OF HAPPINESS, AND THAT'S WHERE WE'VE HEADED WITH OUR *BEST OF BRIDGE 5-INGREDIENT COOKING*. GOOD FOOD PARED DOWN CAN BE TASTY, LESS FUSSY AND STILL FULL OF FLAVOR.

EACH RECIPE WAS DEVELOPED AND TESTED USING JUST FIVE MAIN INGREDIENTS, PLUS "FREE PASS," OR FREEBIE, INGREDIENTS THAT ARE STAPLES IN MOST PEOPLE'S KITCHENS. SALT, BLACK PEPPER, WATER AND OILS LIKE CANOLA OR OLIVE OIL DON'T COUNT IN THE MAIN INGREDIENTS. GETTING A MEAL ON THE TABLE USING ONLY FIVE MAIN INGREDIENTS MEANS YOU HAVE A SHORTER GROCERY LIST AND YOU SPEND LESS TIME PULLING INGREDIENTS TOGETHER. AND ALL THE INGREDIENTS ARE READILY AVAILABLE AT MOST SUPERMARKETS.

AS HOME ECONOMISTS AND AS MOTHERS, WE KNOW WHAT IT'S LIKE TO TRY TO PULL A MEAL TOGETHER WHILE BALANCING FAMILY AND WORK SCHEDULES. WE'VE COMBINED FRESH INGREDIENTS ALONG WITH THE HELP OF STORE-BOUGHT PREPARED AND SEMI-PREPARED INGREDIENTS THAT WE LIKE TO CALL SHORTCUTS. MANY OF THE RECIPES USE FAMILIAR TIME-SAVING INGREDIENTS, SUCH AS PESTO, BOTTLED SAUCES, FROZEN PEROGIES, FROZEN VEGETABLES AND CANNED LEGUMES FOR MAXIMUM FLAVOR AND CONVENIENCE.

THERE ARE PLENTY OF RECIPES IN THIS BOOK THAT YOUR FAMILY WILL LOVE TO MAKE — AND WITH SO FEW INGREDIENTS, IT WON'T BE VERY HARD TO GET THEM INTO THE KITCHEN.

WHETHER THEY ARE JUST STARTING OUT IN THE KITCHEN OR READY TO HEAD OUT ON THEIR OWN, YOUR FAMILY WILL MAKE MANY OF THESE RECIPES THEIR FAVORITES AND LEARN HOW EASY THEY ARE TO MAKE AGAIN AND AGAIN.

IF YOU HAVE THE TIME, WE'VE ALSO INCLUDED RECIPES FOR SOME OF THE BASICS. YOU HAVE THE OPTION TO USE STORE-BOUGHT HELPERS AND, WHEN YOU HAVE MORE TIME, TO MAKE SOME FOODS — LIKE MEATBALLS AND PASTA SAUCE — FROM SCRATCH. WE SUGGEST THAT IF YOU'RE MAKING OUR BASICS, YOU DOUBLE THE RECIPE, SO YOU'LL HAVE THEM HANDY IN THE FRIDGE OR FREEZER TO STREAMLINE YOUR MEAL PREPARATION. MAKE ONCE, EAT TWICE!

WE HOPE YOU ENJOY TRYING OUT THESE RECIPES — THEY'RE SIMPLE TO SHOP FOR AND MAKE FOR A LIGHTER GROCERY BAG. IT ALSO THRILLS US TO SEE PEOPLE CONNECTING AS THEY PREPARE AND ENJOY MEALS TOGETHER. POST YOUR PHOTOS OF THE RECIPES YOU'VE MADE FROM YOUR *BEST OF BRIDGE 5-INGREDIENT COOKING* AND REMEMBER TO TAG US ON INSTAGRAM @BESTOFBRIDGE AND ON FACEBOOK. WE BELIEVE THAT FOOD IS ONE OF THE LANGUAGES OF LOVE!

ENJOY!

—SYLVIA AND EMILY

YOU ONLY LIVE ONCE.
LICK THE BOWL!

BREAKFAST AND BRUNCH

BLENDER BANANA OATMEAL PANCAKES

IF YOU HAVE AN ABUNDANCE OF RIPE BANANAS, MAKING THESE PANCAKES IS A PERFECT WAY TO ENJOY THEM. THE BANANAS PROVIDE EXTRA FLAVOR AND NATURAL SWEETNESS, WHILE THE OATMEAL HAS A MILD NUTTY FLAVOR. ALL THE INGREDIENTS GO INTO THE BLENDER, SO THEY'RE A SNAP TO WHIP UP.

1 CUP	RIPE MASHED BANANAS (ABOUT 3 MEDIUM)	250 ML
2	LARGE EGGS	2
1 CUP	VANILLA ALMOND MILK	250 ML
2 CUPS	OLD-FASHIONED ROLLED OATS	500 ML
2 TSP	BAKING POWDER	10 ML
$1/4$ TSP	SALT	1 ML

IN A BLENDER, PLACE BANANAS, EGGS, MILK, OATS, BAKING POWDER AND SALT. BLEND ON HIGH UNTIL SMOOTH, ABOUT 1 TO 2 MINUTES. ALLOW BATTER TO REST 5 MINUTES TO THICKEN SLIGHTLY. MEANWHILE, OIL OR SPRAY A NONSTICK SKILLET OR GRIDDLE WITH COOKING SPRAY AND HEAT OVER MEDIUM-HIGH HEAT. FOR EACH PANCAKE, SCOOP $1/4$ CUP (60 ML) BATTER ONTO SKILLET.

COOK FOR ABOUT 2 TO 3 MINUTES OR UNTIL BUBBLES BEGIN TO APPEAR ON TOP. FLIP PANCAKES OVER AND COOK FOR 1 MINUTE OR UNTIL GOLDEN BROWN. TRANSFER PANCAKES TO A PLATE. REPEAT WITH REMAINING BATTER, SPRAYING PAN AND ADJUSTING HEAT AS NEEDED BETWEEN BATCHES. MAKES ABOUT 14 PANCAKES.

TIP: LEFTOVERS CAN BE STORED IN AN AIRTIGHT CONTAINER AND REFRIGERATED FOR UP TO 3 DAYS, OR IN THE FREEZER FOR UP TO 1 MONTH. REHEAT IN MICROWAVE OR TOASTER OVEN.

TIP: SERVE WITH YOUR FAVORITE TOPPINGS, SUCH AS MAPLE SYRUP, YOGURT, BANANA SLICES, CHOPPED NUTS OR FRESH BERRIES.

WHY DO BANANAS HAVE TO PUT ON
SUNSCREEN BEFORE THEY GO TO THE BEACH?
BECAUSE THEY MIGHT PEEL.

PUMPKIN SPICE BAKED OATMEAL

THE SCENT OF THIS BAKED BREAKFAST IS WONDERFUL. THERE'S NO ACTUAL PUMPKIN IN THIS OATMEAL, BUT IT DOES INCLUDE THOSE DELICIOUS WARM SPICES THAT ARE TRADITIONALLY IN A PUMPKIN PIE. YOU CAN USE STORE-BOUGHT PUMPKIN SPICE MIX OR MAKE A BATCH OF OUR EASY HOMEMADE SPICE MIX (PAGE 209).

1¾ CUPS	OLD-FASHIONED ROLLED OATS	425 ML
1 TBSP	PUMPKIN PIE SPICE MIX	15 ML
1 TSP	BAKING POWDER	5 ML
2 CUPS	WHOLE MILK	500 ML
2	LARGE EGGS, LIGHTLY BEATEN	2

PREHEAT OVEN TO 375°F (190°C). LIGHTLY OIL AN 8- BY 8-INCH (20 BY 20 CM) SQUARE BAKING PAN. IN A LARGE BOWL, COMBINE OATS, SPICE MIX AND BAKING POWDER. ADD MILK AND EGGS; STIR TO COMBINE. POUR MIXTURE INTO PREPARED PAN. BAKE FOR 35 TO 40 MINUTES, UNTIL THE CENTER IS SET. REMOVE FROM OVEN AND LET COOL 5 MINUTES BEFORE SERVING. SERVES 6.

TIP: THE INGREDIENTS CAN BE MIXED, COVERED AND STORED IN THE REFRIGERATOR OVERNIGHT. IN THE MORNING, REMOVE FROM THE FRIDGE WHILE THE OVEN PREHEATS.

TIP: SERVE WITH MAPLE SYRUP, YOGURT OR FRESH FRUIT, IF DESIRED.

BAKED EGG BITES

THESE EGGS LOOK LIKE MINI SOUFFLÉS AS THEY BAKE IN THE OVEN. AS IS TYPICAL OF MOST SOUFFLÉS, THEY DO COLLAPSE WHEN REMOVED FROM THE OVEN, BUT THEY STILL TASTE DELICIOUS. GENOA SALAMI IS A FLAVORFUL ITALIAN CURED SAUSAGE.

I CUP	LIGHTLY PACKED SPINACH, FINELY CHOPPED	250 ML
1/3 CUP	FINELY CHOPPED GENOA SALAMI	75 ML
14	LARGE EGGS	14
1/4 CUP	MILK	60 ML
1/2 TSP	EACH SALT AND BLACK PEPPER	2 ML
3/4 CUP	SHREDDED SHARP (OLD) CHEDDAR CHEESE	175 ML

PREHEAT OVEN TO 350°F (180°C). COAT A 12-CUP MUFFIN PAN WITH COOKING SPRAY. DIVIDE SPINACH AND SALAMI EVENLY AMONG MUFFIN CUPS. IN A LARGE BOWL, WHISK EGGS, MILK, SALT AND PEPPER TOGETHER UNTIL WELL COMBINED. DIVIDE EGG MIXTURE INTO MUFFIN CUPS, THEN SPRINKLE WITH CHEESE. MUFFIN CUPS WILL BE VERY FULL.

BAKE FOR 18 TO 20 MINUTES, JUST UNTIL SET. COOL ON A RACK FOR 2 MINUTES, THEN RUN A KNIFE AROUND EACH EGG BITE TO HELP REMOVE. MAKES 12.

TIP: STORE ANY LEFTOVERS IN THE REFRIGERATOR FOR UP TO 3 DAYS. THESE ARE ALSO GREAT TO PACK FOR LUNCH.

EGG PIZZA

THIS DELICIOUS AND HEALTHY TAKE ON PIZZA
WILL HAVE THE LITTLE KIDS — AND BIG KIDS —
SMILING AND COMING BACK FOR MORE.
IT'S FUN AND QUICK TO MAKE. CUT INTO
WEDGES OR THICK STRIPS FOR EASY DIPPING.

2	LARGE EGGS	2
1/2 TSP	DRIED OREGANO OR BASIL	2 ML
PINCH	SALT	PINCH
8	SLICES PEPPERONI	8
2 TBSP	SHREDDED MOZZARELLA CHEESE	30 ML
3 TBSP	PIZZA OR PASTA SAUCE	45 ML

SPRAY SMALL NONSTICK SKILLET WITH COOKING SPRAY
AND HEAT OVER MEDIUM HEAT.

IN A BOWL, BEAT TOGETHER EGGS, OREGANO AND
SALT; POUR INTO SKILLET AND STIR ONCE. TOP WITH
PEPPERONI AND CHEESE. COVER AND COOK FOR ABOUT
3 MINUTES OR UNTIL EGGS ARE SET AND CHEESE IS
MELTED. SLIDE OUT ONTO PLATE AND SERVE WITH SAUCE.
SERVES 1.

TIP: WARM YOUR PIZZA SAUCE IN THE MICROWAVE, OR
ENJOY IT COLD IF YOU PREFER.

TIP: GET CREATIVE BY COMBINING DIFFERENT MEATS,
CHEESES AND VEGGIES.

VEGETARIAN OPTION: OMIT PEPPERONI AND SUBSTITUTE 3 TBSP (45 ML) DICED RED OR GREEN BELL PEPPER.

MEAT VARIATIONS: TRY USING ABOUT 3 TBSP (45 ML) CHOPPED HAM, TURKEY OR CHICKEN, OR COOKED STRIP OR PEAMEAL BACON OR CRUMBLED COOKED SAUSAGE INSTEAD OF PEPPERONI.

CHEESE VARIATIONS: TRY SHARP (OLD) CHEDDAR, PROVOLONE OR ASIAGO CHEESE INSTEAD OF MOZZARELLA.

WHAT DO SNOWMEN EAT FOR BREAKFAST?
FROSTED FLAKES!

SCRAMBLED EGG NAANS

SCRAMBLE THE EGGS WHILE YOU WARM UP THE NAAN IN THE TOASTER. BREAKFAST CAN BE THAT SIMPLE!

1 TBSP	BUTTER	15 ML
8	LARGE EGGS, BEATEN	8
1/2 TSP	EACH SALT AND BLACK PEPPER	2 ML
1/4 CUP	CHOPPED FRESH PARSLEY OR BASIL	60 ML
4	SMOKED SALMON, HAM OR TURKEY SLICES, CHOPPED	4
4	MINI NAAN BREADS	4

IN A LARGE NONSTICK SKILLET, MELT BUTTER OVER MEDIUM HEAT. POUR IN EGGS, SALT AND PEPPER. COOK, STIRRING FOR ABOUT 2 MINUTES OR UNTIL CREAMY BUT STARTING TO SET. STIR IN PARSLEY AND CONTINUE COOKING FOR ABOUT 3 MINUTES OR UNTIL SET.

MEANWHILE, WARM NAAN BREADS IN THE TOASTER OR OVEN. TOP EACH NAAN WITH SOME OF THE SCRAMBLED EGGS AND SMOKED SALMON. SERVES 4.

TIP: WANT SOME CHEESE WITH YOUR EGGS? OMIT SMOKED SALMON AND TOP THE NAAN WITH A CHEESE SLICE BEFORE ADDING EGGS — WHICH ALSO MAKES IT VEGETARIAN!

SMOKED SALMON FRITTATA

A QUICK AND SIMPLE BREAKFAST OR BRUNCH FOR ANY DAY OF THE WEEK. THE TANGY FRESH GOAT CHEESE ADDS A WONDERFUL CREAMY TEXTURE TO THIS DISH. BE SURE TO SPREAD THE TOPPING EVENLY SO EACH BITE IS RICH AND DELICIOUS.

4	LARGE EGGS	4
1 TBSP	WATER	15 ML
1/4 TSP	BLACK PEPPER	1 ML
1 TBSP	CANOLA OIL	15 ML
1/3 CUP	CHOPPED SMOKED SALMON	75 ML
1	GREEN ONION, CHOPPED	1
1/2 CUP	CRUMBLED GOAT CHEESE	125 ML
1 TBSP	CHOPPED FRESH DILL	15 ML

IN A SMALL BOWL, WHISK TOGETHER EGGS, WATER AND PEPPER. IN A MEDIUM NONSTICK SKILLET, HEAT OIL OVER MEDIUM HEAT. POUR IN EGG MIXTURE; COOK FOR 1 MINUTE. AS IT COOKS, RUN A RUBBER SPATULA AROUND THE EDGE TO ALLOW UNCOOKED EGG TO SLIDE UNDERNEATH. SPRINKLE SALMON, ONION, CHEESE AND DILL OVER TOP. COVER SKILLET AND COOK 3 MINUTES OR UNTIL TOP IS ALMOST SET. SERVES 2.

TIP: SERVE WITH TOASTED BAGELS OR YOUR FAVORITE BREAD.

TIP: IF FRESH DILL IS NOT AVAILABLE, SUBSTITUTE WITH 1 TSP (5 ML) DRIED DILL.

QUINOA BREAKFAST BURRITOS

BURRITOS ARE ALWAYS A FAVORITE TO TAKE AWAY.
WHY NOT MAKE YOUR OWN AT HOME AND HAVE
THEM AT THE READY ALONG WITH YOUR LATTE
FOR A LESS EXPENSIVE ON-THE-GO OPTION!

1 1/4 CUPS	WATER	300 ML
1/2 TSP	SALT	2 ML
3/4 CUP	QUINOA	175 ML
1/2 TSP	BLACK PEPPER	2 ML
3/4 CUP	SHREDDED SHARP (OLD) CHEDDAR CHEESE	175 ML
2/3 CUP	DICED BLACK FOREST HAM, TURKEY OR CHICKEN	150 ML
1/2 CUP	SALSA	125 ML
4	LARGE FLOUR TORTILLAS	4

IN A SAUCEPAN, BRING WATER AND SALT TO BOIL.
ADD QUINOA AND REDUCE HEAT; SIMMER FOR ABOUT
12 MINUTES OR UNTIL QUINOA IS TENDER. COVER AND
SET ASIDE FOR 5 MINUTES. FLUFF WITH FORK AND STIR
IN PEPPER.

IN A LARGE BOWL, COMBINE CHEESE, HAM AND SALSA.
ADD QUINOA AND GENTLY TOSS MIXTURE TOGETHER.
DIVIDE MIXTURE AMONG FLOUR TORTILLAS, PLACING IN
THE CENTER OF EACH TORTILLA. FOLD IN TWO SIDES
AND ROLL UP. SERVES 4.

MAKE AHEAD: WRAP EACH BURRITO INDIVIDUALLY AND REFRIGERATE FOR UP TO 2 DAYS OR FREEZE FOR UP TO 2 WEEKS. POP IN THE MICROWAVE TO WARM THROUGH BEFORE ENJOYING. THAW FROM FREEZER BEFORE REHEATING.

TIP: IF YOU ENJOY A CRUNCHY EXTERIOR, TRY PAN-FRYING YOUR BURRITOS IN A SKILLET PREPARED WITH COOKING SPRAY.

VEGETARIAN OPTION: INSTEAD OF HAM, ADD YOUR FAVORITE CANNED BEANS OR VEGGIE MEAT SUBSTITUTE TO THE FILLING.

CHIPS AND SALSA ARE IN A SERIOUS RELATION-CHIP.

SPANISH CHORIZO TORTILLA

YOU CAN MAKE THIS AHEAD AND WARM IT IN THE
OVEN OR SIMPLY SERVE IT AT ROOM TEMPERATURE.

2 TBSP	CANOLA OIL	30 ML
4	SMALL YELLOW-FLESHED POTATOES (ABOUT I LB/500 G), CUT INTO $1/2$ INCH (I CM) PIECES	4
2	SMALL SHALLOTS, FINELY CHOPPED	2
$1/2$ CUP	WATER	125 ML
I	PACKAGE (8 OZ/250 G) SEMI-DRIED CHORIZO SAUSAGE, SLICED	I
8	LARGE EGGS	8
$1/2$ TSP	EACH SALT AND BLACK PEPPER	2 ML
$1/2$ CUP	SHREDDED MANCHEGO OR GRATED PARMESAN CHEESE	125 ML

IN A LARGE OVENPROOF NONSTICK SKILLET, HEAT
OIL OVER MEDIUM-HIGH HEAT AND SAUTÉ POTATOES
AND SHALLOTS FOR 5 MINUTES, STIRRING OFTEN. ADD
WATER, REDUCE HEAT TO MEDIUM-LOW AND COVER
AND COOK FOR ABOUT IO MINUTES OR UNTIL POTATOES
ARE FORK-TENDER. UNCOVER AND ADD CHORIZO; COOK,
STIRRING FOR 2 MINUTES.

MEANWHILE, PREHEAT OVEN TO 400°F (200°C). IN A
LARGE BOWL, WHISK TOGETHER EGGS, SALT AND PEPPER
AND POUR INTO SKILLET. INCREASE HEAT TO MEDIUM
AND COOK, LIFTING THE EDGE WITH A RUBBER SPATULA
TO ALLOW UNCOOKED EGG TO SLIDE UNDERNEATH, FOR
ABOUT 3 MINUTES OR UNTIL BOTTOM IS LIGHT GOLDEN
AND SIDES ARE STARTING TO SET.

PLACE SKILLET IN OVEN AND BAKE FOR ABOUT
10 MINUTES OR UNTIL KNIFE INSERTED IN CENTER COMES
OUT CLEAN. SPRINKLE WITH CHEESE AND BROIL FOR ABOUT
2 MINUTES OR UNTIL GOLDEN ON TOP. SERVES 4 TO 6.

I'VE JUST WRITTEN A SONG ABOUT TORTILLAS
— ACTUALLY, IT'S MORE OF A WRAP.

BREAKFAST SAUSAGE PATTIES

HOMEMADE SAUSAGE PATTIES CAN'T BE BEAT FOR FLAVOR. WE'VE LEFT THE FENNEL SEED WHOLE FOR TASTE AND TEXTURE. THE PATTIES ARE PERFECT SERVED WITH A SIDE OF POTATOES AND JUST AS DELICIOUS TUCKED INTO A BREAKFAST SANDWICH.

2 TSP	ITALIAN SEASONING	10 ML
2 TSP	PAPRIKA	10 ML
1 TSP	ONION POWDER	5 ML
1/2 TSP	FENNEL SEEDS	2 ML
1/2 TSP	EACH SALT AND BLACK PEPPER	2 ML
1 LB	LEAN GROUND PORK	500 G

PREHEAT OVEN TO 350°F (180°C); SET ASIDE A PARCHMENT-LINED RIMMED BAKING SHEET. IN A MEDIUM BOWL, COMBINE ITALIAN SEASONING, PAPRIKA, ONION POWDER, FENNEL SEEDS, SALT AND PEPPER. ADD PORK AND MIX UNTIL WELL COMBINED. (HANDS WORK BEST FOR MIXING!) SHAPE INTO 8 PATTIES, ABOUT 1/2-INCH (1 CM) THICK AND PLACE ON PREPARED BAKING SHEET.

BAKE FOR 15 TO 20 MINUTES, OR UNTIL CENTER IS NO LONGER PINK INSIDE. SERVES 4.

TIP: COOKED PATTIES CAN BE STORED IN THE REFRIGERATOR FOR UP TO 4 DAYS, OR FROZEN FOR UP TO 2 MONTHS.

APPETIZERS

PIMENTO CHEESE

PIMENTO CHEESE IS A RETRO CLASSIC THAT IS STILL LOVED. YOU CAN USE PRE-SHREDDED CHEDDAR CHEESE, BUT FRESHLY SHREDDED CHEESE WILL YIELD A CREAMIER RESULT. SERVE WITH YOUR FAVORITE CRACKERS OR RAW VEGETABLES AS A DIP.

8 OZ	BRICK-STYLE CREAM CHEESE, CUBED AND SOFTENED	250 G
1/4 CUP	MAYONNAISE	60 ML
I TSP	WORCESTERSHIRE SAUCE	5 ML
2 CUPS	SHREDDED SHARP (OLD) CHEDDAR CHEESE	500 ML
1/4 CUP	DICED PIMENTOS, WELL DRAINED	60 ML
1/4 TSP	EACH SALT AND BLACK PEPPER	I ML

IN A LARGE BOWL, USING AN ELECTRIC MIXER, COMBINE CREAM CHEESE AND MAYONNAISE. ADD WORCESTERSHIRE, CHEDDAR CHEESE, PIMENTOS, SALT AND PEPPER AND MIX UNTIL WELL COMBINED AND FLUFFY. ADD ADDITIONAL SALT AND PEPPER, IF DESIRED. TRANSFER TO A SERVING DISH. LEFTOVERS CAN BE REFRIGERATED FOR UP TO 5 DAYS. MAKES ABOUT 2 1/2 CUPS (625 ML).

TIP: THIS CHEESE IS SO VERSATILE — EXPERIMENT AND ENJOY IN A GRILLED CHEESE SANDWICH, STIRRED INTO MACARONI AND CHEESE, SPREAD ON A BURGER, SLATHERED ON A FRESH HOT BISCUIT AND WITH ANY OTHER FOOD YOU CAN THINK OF!

SMOKED SALMON DEVILED EGGS

YOU CAN GET FANCY AND PIPE THE EGG YOLK MIXTURE BACK INTO THE WHITES, OR SIMPLY SCOOP THE MIXTURE USING A SPOON. EITHER WAY, THESE DEVILED EGGS ARE GOING TO GET EATEN UP VERY QUICKLY!

2 TBSP	MAYONNAISE	30 ML
2 TSP	DIJON MUSTARD	10 ML
1 TBSP	CHOPPED FRESH DILL	15 ML
8	LARGE HARD-COOKED EGGS, PEELED	8
1/4 CUP	FINELY CHOPPED SMOKED SALMON	60 ML
	SALT AND BLACK PEPPER	

IN A MEDIUM BOWL, COMBINE MAYONNAISE, MUSTARD AND DILL. SLICE EGGS IN HALF LENGTHWISE AND SCOOP OUT THE YOLKS, MASHING THEM INTO THE MAYONNAISE MIXTURE. SET EGG WHITES ON A SERVING PLATTER, CUT SIDE UP. STIR SALMON INTO YOLK MIXTURE; SEASON WITH SALT AND PEPPER TO TASTE.

SPOON OR PIPE MIXTURE INTO EGG WHITE HALVES, MOUNDING THE FILLING. GARNISH WITH ADDITIONAL DILL AND SMOKED SALMON, IF DESIRED. SERVES 8.

TIP: DEVILED EGGS CAN BE MADE UP TO 1 DAY IN ADVANCE. REFRIGERATE AND STORE IN A COVERED CONTAINER.

SCOTCH EGGS

THESE FAVORITES ARE PERFECT TO MAKE
AHEAD AND FRY UP LATER WHEN YOU CAN SERVE
THEM CUT IN HALF FOR EVERYONE TO ENJOY.
FOR A DELICIOUS TOPPING, SERVE THEM
WITH MUSTARD OR ZUCCHINI RELISH.

I LB	MILD OR SPICY ITALIAN SAUSAGE MEAT	500 G
12	HARD-COOKED LARGE EGGS, PEELED	12
1/3 CUP	ALL-PURPOSE FLOUR	75 ML
2	LARGE EGGS, LIGHTLY BEATEN	2
1/4 TSP	EACH SALT AND BLACK PEPPER	I ML
I CUP	SEASONED PANKO BREAD CRUMBS	250 ML
	CANOLA OIL	

PREHEAT OVEN TO 400°F (200°C). DIVIDE SAUSAGE
MIXTURE INTO 12 BALLS AND FLATTEN WELL. PLACE
HARD-COOKED EGG IN CENTER AND WRAP AND PRESS
SAUSAGE AROUND EGG FIRMLY. REPEAT WITH REMAINING
EGGS AND SAUSAGE. PLACE THE FLOUR IN ONE SHALLOW
BOWL. IN ANOTHER SHALLOW BOWL, WHISK EGGS WITH
SALT AND PEPPER. IN A THIRD SHALLOW DISH, ADD BREAD
CRUMBS. DIP EACH SAUSAGE-WRAPPED EGG INTO FLOUR,
COATING COMPLETELY, THEN INTO EGG, LETTING EXCESS
DRIP OFF. FINALLY, COAT THE EGG IN BREAD CRUMBS AND
PLACE ON PARCHMENT PAPER-LINED BAKING SHEET.

BAKE EGGS FOR 10 MINUTES OR UNTIL SAUSAGE IS SET.
REMOVE FROM OVEN AND LET COOL COMPLETELY. (COVER
AND REFRIGERATE FOR UP TO 3 DAYS BEFORE FRYING.)

IN A SAUCEPAN WITH HIGH SIDES, HEAT ABOUT 4 INCHES (10 CM) OF CANOLA OIL TO 350°F (180°C). FRY EGGS IN BATCHES FOR ABOUT 3 MINUTES OR UNTIL DEEP GOLDEN BROWN. DRAIN ON PAPER TOWEL-LINED PLATE. SLICE EACH IN HALF LENGTHWISE BEFORE SERVING. MAKES 24.

HOW TO HARD-COOK EGGS: PLACE EGGS IN A SINGLE LAYER IN SAUCEPAN AND COVER WITH WATER, ABOUT 2 INCHES (5 CM) OVER TOP OF EGGS. BRING TO A BOIL. REMOVE FROM HEAT; COVER AND LET STAND FOR 10 MINUTES. DRAIN AND COOL EGGS IN COLD WATER. WHEN EASY TO HANDLE, CRACK SHELLS AND PEEL, USING WATER TO HELP REMOVE ANY SMALL SHELL PIECES IF NEEDED.

TIP: YOU CAN SUBSTITUTE SAUSAGES FOR THE SAUSAGE MEAT; SIMPLY REMOVE THE CASINGS FROM THE SAUSAGES BEFORE USING.

TIP: YOU CAN SUBSTITUTE REGULAR SEASONED BREAD CRUMBS FOR THE PANKO VERSION.

TIP: FOR A GLUTEN-FREE OPTION, SUBSTITUTE GLUTEN-FREE FLOUR AND BREAD CRUMBS AND LOOK FOR GLUTEN-FREE SAUSAGE MEAT.

JAMES'S SAUSAGE-STUFFED JALAPEÑO PEPPERS

THESE SPICY LITTLE POPPERS ARE GREAT DONE ON THE GRILL OR SMOKER FOR BACKYARD SUMMER GET-TOGETHERS. IF YOU WANT TO MAKE THEM YEAR ROUND, CHECK OUT OUR OVEN VARIATION. SOME JALAPEÑO PEPPERS ARE HOTTER THAN OTHERS, SO YOU MAY WANT TO STICK TO A MILD SAUSAGE FILLING FIRST TIME OUT AND SEE HOW YOU FARE.

12	JALAPEÑO PEPPERS	12
8 OZ	MILD OR SPICY ITALIAN SAUSAGE MEAT OR SAUSAGES, CASINGS REMOVED	250 G
1 CUP	SHREDDED CHEDDAR AND MOZZARELLA CHEESE MIX	250 ML
1/4 CUP	SEASONED BREAD CRUMBS	60 ML
12	UNCOOKED BACON SLICES, CUT IN HALF	12

CUT JALAPEÑO PEPPERS IN HALF LENGTHWISE AND REMOVE SEEDS. PLACE PEPPERS CUT SIDE UP ON BAKING SHEET; SET ASIDE. PREHEAT GRILL TO MEDIUM HEAT. IN A BOWL, COMBINE SAUSAGE MEAT, CHEESE AND BREAD CRUMBS. DIVIDE MIXTURE AMONG PEPPERS. WRAP EACH PEPPER IN HALF A BACON SLICE AND RETURN TO BAKING SHEET.

USING TONGS, PLACE STUFFED PEPPERS ONTO GRILL. CLOSE LID AND COOK FOR ABOUT 15 MINUTES, TURNING ONCE OR UNTIL BACON IS CRISP AND SAUSAGE IS NO LONGER PINK INSIDE. MAKES 24.

TIP: BE SURE TO WEAR GLOVES WHEN YOU'RE SEEDING THE PEPPERS TO AVOID A BURNING SENSATION LATER IN THE DAY.

SMOKED VARIATION: SET SMOKER TO 300°F (150°C) AND PLACE PEPPERS ON GRILL. CLOSE LID AND SMOKE FOR ABOUT 30 MINUTES OR UNTIL BACON IS CRISP AND SAUSAGE IS NO LONGER PINK INSIDE.

OVEN VARIATION: BAKE PEPPERS IN 375°F (190°C) OVEN FOR ABOUT 20 MINUTES OR UNTIL BACON IS CRISP AND SAUSAGE IS NO LONGER PINK INSIDE.

MINI PEPPER VARIATION: IF YOU DON'T WANT THE HEAT, PICK UP BAGS OF MINI PEPPERS AND USE THOSE IN PLACE OF THE JALAPEÑO PEPPERS.

FIG JAM AND GOAT CHEESE TART

THIS VERSATILE APPETIZER CAN ALSO BE SERVED ALONGSIDE A GREEN SALAD AND ENJOYED AS A LIGHT LUNCH. FIG JAM IS USUALLY LOCATED IN THE INTERNATIONAL SECTION OF THE GROCERY STORE.

2	ONIONS, THINLY SLICED	2
2 TBSP	CANOLA OIL	30 ML
8 OZ	FROZEN PUFF PASTRY, THAWED	250 G
1/3 CUP	FIG JAM	75 ML
4 OZ	SOFT GOAT CHEESE, CRUMBLED	100 G
1/2 TSP	DRIED THYME	2 ML
1/4 TSP	EACH SALT AND BLACK PEPPER	1 ML

PREHEAT OVEN TO 425°F (220°C). IN A LARGE SKILLET, OVER MEDIUM-HIGH HEAT, ADD ONIONS AND OIL. COOK AND STIR FOR 5 MINUTES. REDUCE HEAT TO MEDIUM AND CONTINUE COOKING ABOUT 10 MINUTES UNTIL ONIONS ARE CARAMEL IN COLOR AND SOFT; SET ASIDE TO COOL. ON A PARCHMENT PAPER-LINED BAKING SHEET, LAY OUT PUFF PASTRY AND ROLL INTO A 10- BY 10-INCH (25 BY 25 CM) SQUARE. SPREAD JAM OVER TOP OF PASTRY, LEAVING A 1/2-INCH (1 CM) BORDER. SPRINKLE ONIONS, CHEESE, THYME, SALT AND PEPPER OVER TOP.

BAKE TART FOR 20 TO 25 MINUTES, OR UNTIL THE PASTRY HAS PUFFED UP AROUND THE EDGES AND IS GOLDEN BROWN. COOL SLIGHTLY, THEN CUT INTO PIECES. SERVES 6.

TIP: MOST PACKAGES OF FROZEN PUFF PASTRY COME IN A 1-LB (500 G) SIZE; YOU USE ONLY HALF A PACKAGE FOR THIS RECIPE.

TIP: NEED SOME IDEAS TO USE UP THE EXTRA FIG JAM? IT'S GREAT SERVED WITH CHEESE AND CRACKERS, AND WITH GRILLED MEATS, AND SPREAD IN A SANDWICH.

TIP: FIG JAM IS AVAILABLE IN MANY VARIATIONS. SOME INCLUDE INGREDIENTS SUCH AS NUTS, ANISE, CARDAMOM, ROSE WATER AND ORANGE BLOSSOM WATER. CHECK THE INGREDIENT LABEL BEFORE PURCHASING.

TIP: DOUBLE THE RECIPE AND MAKE TWO TARTS FOR A LARGER GET-TOGETHER.

MAKE AHEAD: YOU CAN PREPARE THE TART THE NIGHT BEFORE. COVER AND STORE IN THE REFRIGERATOR. BAKE AS DIRECTED THE NEXT DAY.

TWO CHEESE TRUCKS RAN INTO EACH OTHER.
DE BRIE WAS EVERYWHERE.

EGGPLANT TACOS

USING EGGPLANT FOR THE SHELL ADDS MORE VEGGIE BITE TO THIS TACO AND FEWER CARBS. TRY THIS FUN WAY TO ENJOY TACOS WITH AN ITALIAN TWIST. EMILY'S FRIEND KATE SUGGESTS SERVING THEM UP TOSTADA STYLE, TO ENJOY WITH FORK AND KNIFE.

2	SMALL EGGPLANTS (ABOUT 1 LB/500 G TOTAL), TRIMMED	2
3 TBSP	EXTRA VIRGIN OLIVE OIL	45 ML
1/2 TSP	EACH SALT AND BLACK PEPPER, DIVIDED	2 ML
1 1/2 CUPS	RICOTTA CHEESE OR HUMMUS	375 ML
1/4 CUP	DICED SUN-DRIED TOMATOES IN OIL	60 ML
1/4 CUP	CHOPPED FRESH BASIL	60 ML
1 CUP	BABY ARUGULA	250 ML

PREHEAT GRILL TO MEDIUM-HIGH. SLICE EACH EGGPLANT CROSSWISE INTO 12 CIRCLES. TOSS WITH OIL AND HALF OF EACH OF THE SALT AND PEPPER. PLACE ON GREASED GRILL FOR ABOUT 10 MINUTES, TURNING ONCE, UNTIL GOLDEN AND TENDER. REMOVE TO PLATTER AND SET ASIDE.

IN A BOWL, STIR TOGETHER CHEESE, TOMATOES AND BASIL WITH REMAINING SALT AND PEPPER. DIVIDE AMONG EGGPLANT SLICES, FOLDING THEM INTO A TACO SHAPE TO HOLD THE FILLING. TOP EACH WITH SOME OF THE ARUGULA TO SERVE. MAKES ABOUT 24 PIECES.

TIP: IF YOU FIND THE EGGPLANT TACOS ARE NOT STAYING FOLDED, USE A TOOTHPICK TO HOLD THEM TOGETHER.

PAN-FRY VARIATION: SPRAY NONSTICK SKILLET AND PAN-FRY EGGPLANT SLICES IN BATCHES OVER MEDIUM HEAT FOR ABOUT 8 MINUTES, TURNING ONCE, UNTIL GOLDEN.

OVEN ROASTED VARIATION: LAY EGGPLANT SLICES ON PARCHMENT PAPER-LINED BAKING SHEET AND ROAST IN 400°F (200°C) OVEN FOR ABOUT 12 MINUTES, TURNING ONCE, UNTIL GOLDEN AND TENDER.

A SMALL KITCHEN MAKES THE HOUSE BIG.
—ITALIAN PROVERB

HOMEMADE SEED CRACKERS

IT'S HARD TO STOP EATING THESE CRISP,
FLAVORFUL CRACKERS! WHO KNEW
THAT HOMEMADE COULD BE SO EASY?

1/2 CUP	PUMPKIN SEEDS	125 ML
1/2 CUP	CHIA SEEDS	125 ML
1/2 CUP	SESAME SEEDS	125 ML
1/2 CUP	GROUND FLAX SEED	125 ML
2 TSP	ITALIAN SEASONING	10 ML
1/4 TSP	SALT	1 ML
1 1/4 CUPS	WATER	300 ML

IN A MEDIUM BOWL, COMBINE ALL INGREDIENTS AND LET SIT FOR 5 MINUTES FOR MIXTURE TO BEGIN TO MELD TOGETHER. MEANWHILE, PREHEAT OVEN TO 350°F (180°C) AND LINE TWO BAKING SHEETS WITH PARCHMENT PAPER. STIR THE SEED MIXTURE AND DIVIDE ONTO PREPARED BAKING SHEETS. SPREAD THE MIXTURE INTO ROUGHLY AN 11- BY 11-INCH (27.5 BY 27.5 CM) SQUARE ON EACH SHEET.

BAKE FOR 25 MINUTES, ROTATE PANS, THEN BAKE AN ADDITIONAL 25 MINUTES OR UNTIL CRISP. REMOVE FROM OVEN, COOL AND THEN BREAK INTO SMALLER PIECES. SERVES 8.

TIP: STORE IN AN AIRTIGHT CONTAINER FOR UP TO 2 WEEKS.

CURRIED SWEET PECANS

SWEET AND MILDLY SPICED, THESE PECANS ARE PERFECT FOR MUNCHING. MAKE EXTRA FOR A WELCOMED FOOD GIFT ANY TIME OF THE YEAR.

3 CUPS	WHOLE PECANS	750 ML
1	LARGE EGG WHITE	1
1/3 CUP	GRANULATED SUGAR	75 ML
1 1/2 TSP	CURRY POWDER	7 ML
1 TSP	SALT	5 ML
1/2 TSP	GARLIC POWDER	2 ML

PREHEAT OVEN TO 275°F (140°C). LINE A RIMMED BAKING SHEET WITH PARCHMENT PAPER. IN A MEDIUM BOWL, WHISK EGG WHITE UNTIL FROTHY, THEN WHISK IN SUGAR, CURRY POWDER, SALT AND GARLIC POWDER. ADD NUTS AND TOSS TO EVENLY COAT.

SPREAD PECANS OUT IN SINGLE LAYER ON PREPARED BAKING SHEET AND ROAST FOR 30 TO 35 MINUTES. SEPARATE ANY PECANS THAT ARE STUCK TOGETHER, THEN COOL COMPLETELY. STORE IN AN AIRTIGHT CONTAINER FOR UP TO 1 WEEK. MAKES 3 CUPS (750 ML).

TIP: TRY COARSELY CHOPPING THESE PECANS TO SERVE ON TOP OF A SALAD.

DOUBLE CHEESE POLENTA FRIES

THIS POPULAR RESTAURANT APPETIZER IS NOW EASY TO ENJOY AT HOME! THESE CORNMEAL-BASE FRIES ARE A FUN AND EASY-TO-PICK-UP APPETIZER. EMILY JOINED HER MOM IN ENJOYING SECOND HELPINGS OF THESE TASTY FRIES!

4 CUPS	WATER	1 L
1$\frac{1}{2}$ TSP	SALT	7 ML
1$\frac{1}{2}$ CUPS	CORNMEAL	375 ML
1 CUP	SHREDDED SHARP (OLD) CHEDDAR CHEESE	250 ML
2 TBSP	CHOPPED FRESH BASIL OR PARSLEY	30 ML
$\frac{1}{4}$ TSP	BLACK PEPPER	1 ML
	CANOLA OIL	
$\frac{1}{2}$ CUP	FRESH GRATED PARMESAN CHEESE	125 ML
1 CUP	MARINARA SAUCE, SALSA OR GARLIC AIOLI	250 ML

IN A SAUCEPAN, BRING WATER AND SALT TO BOIL. WHISK IN CORNMEAL UNTIL SMOOTH. REDUCE HEAT TO MEDIUM-LOW AND, USING A WOODEN SPOON, COOK STIRRING FOR ABOUT 10 MINUTES OR UNTIL VERY THICK. REMOVE FROM HEAT AND STIR IN CHEESE, PARSLEY AND PEPPER. SCRAPE ONTO AN OILED 13- BY 10-INCH (32 BY 25 CM) BAKING SHEET AND REFRIGERATE FOR AT LEAST 4 HOURS OR UNTIL FIRM AND COLD.

MEANWHILE, HEAT ABOUT 4 INCHES (10 CM) OF OIL IN DEEP SAUCEPAN OR DEEP FRYER TO 350°F (180°C). TURN OUT FIRM POLENTA ONTO LARGE CUTTING BOARD. USING A CHEF'S KNIFE, CUT IN HALF LENGTHWISE AND THEN CUT ACROSS INTO 1-INCH (2.5 CM) THICK FINGERS.

DEEP-FRY POLENTA FRIES IN BATCHES FOR ABOUT 3 MINUTES OR UNTIL LIGHT GOLDEN BROWN. REMOVE WITH SLOTTED SPOON TO PAPER TOWEL-LINED PLATE AND SPRINKLE WITH CHEESE. SERVE WITH MARINARA SAUCE FOR DIPPING. MAKES ABOUT 24 FRIES (4 TO 6 SERVINGS)

BAKED VARIATION: OMIT FRYING STEP AND PLACE POLENTA FINGERS ON PARCHMENT PAPER-LINED BAKING SHEET. BRUSH WITH OIL ON BOTH SIDES AND BAKE IN 450°F (220°C) OVEN FOR ABOUT 20 MINUTES, TURNING HALFWAY, UNTIL GOLDEN AND CRISP.

GIVING UP CARBS?
OVER MY BREAD BODY!

GOAT CHEESE AND PEAR BITES

THIS CRANBERRY AND GOAT CHEESE COMBINATION
BLENDS PERFECTLY FOR A WARM APPETIZER ON
A COLD WINTER NIGHT. CREAMY GOAT CHEESE
WRAPPED IN CRISPY PHYLLO CAN ALSO BE
SAVORED WITH SPARKLING WINE OR A COCKTAIL.

1	PACKAGE (8 OZ/250 G) CRANBERRY AND CINNAMON GOAT CHEESE	1
1	SMALL, RIPE BUT FIRM BARTLETT OR BOSC PEAR, CORED AND FINELY DICED	1
1/4 CUP	DRIED CRANBERRIES OR FINELY CHOPPED WALNUTS	60 ML
PINCH	EACH SALT AND BLACK PEPPER	PINCH
8	SHEETS PHYLLO PASTRY	8
1/3 CUP	BUTTER, MELTED	75 ML

IN A BOWL, STIR TOGETHER GOAT CHEESE, PEAR,
CRANBERRIES, SALT AND PEPPER UNTIL COMBINED
AND SET ASIDE. PREHEAT OVEN TO 400°F (200°C).

LAY ONE SHEET OF PHYLLO ON WORK SURFACE AND
BRUSH LIGHTLY WITH BUTTER. TOP WITH ANOTHER SHEET
OF PHYLLO AND BRUSH WITH BUTTER. REPEAT WITH
ANOTHER TWO SHEETS OF PHYLLO AND BUTTER UNTIL
FOUR SHEETS HAVE BEEN USED. SPOON HALF OF THE
GOAT CHEESE MIXTURE ALONG ONE LONG SIDE OF PHYLLO,
LEAVING A 2-INCH (5 CM) BORDER ON EACH SIDE. FOLD
OVER SIDES AND ROLL UP PHYLLO JELLYROLL STYLE TO
FORM A LONG ROLL. PLACE WITH SEAM SIDE DOWN ON A
LARGE PARCHMENT PAPER-LINED BAKING SHEET. REPEAT
WITH REMAINING PHYLLO AND FILLING. BRUSH ROLLS WITH

BUTTER AND SCORE TOP OF PHYLLO AT ABOUT 1 INCH (2.5 CM) INTERVALS.

BAKE FOR ABOUT 15 MINUTES OR UNTIL GOLDEN BROWN. LET COOL FOR 20 MINUTES. USING A SERRATED KNIFE, SLICE INTO 1-INCH (2.5 CM) THICK ROUNDS. MAKES ABOUT 30 PIECES.

TIP: WHEN WORKING WITH PHYLLO PASTRY, USE ONE SHEET AT TIME AND KEEP THE REMAINING SHEETS COVERED UNDER A LIGHTLY DAMPENED TOWEL TO PREVENT THE PASTRY FROM DRYING OUT.

VARIATION: TO SERVE AS A FIRST COURSE, CUT EACH LOG INTO SIX PIECES AND SERVE ON A BED OF MIXED GREENS TOSSED WITH A LIGHT OIL AND WHITE WINE VINEGAR DRESSING.

VARIATION: BLUEBERRY GOAT CHEESE: LOOK FOR OTHER FRUITED GOAT CHEESE COMBINATIONS LIKE BLUEBERRY TO SUBSTITUTE FOR THE CRANBERRY GOAT CHEESE. APPLE CINNAMON IS ANOTHER ONE TO LOOK OUT FOR.

PROSCIUTTO-WRAPPED ASPARAGUS WITH BLUE CHEESE DIP

BE SURE TO SERVE THE ASPARAGUS RIGHT OFF THE GRILL WHILE ENJOYING DRINKS ON THE DECK.

BLUE CHEESE DIP

1/3 CUP	MAYONNAISE	75 ML
1/4 CUP	CRUMBLED BLUE CHEESE	60 ML
2 TBSP	EXTRA VIRGIN OLIVE OIL	30 ML
1 TBSP	LEMON JUICE	15 ML
PINCH	BLACK PEPPER	PINCH

PROSCIUTTO-WRAPPED ASPARAGUS

24	THICK SPEARS ASPARAGUS	24
1 TBSP	EXTRA VIRGIN OLIVE OIL	15 ML
12	THIN SLICES PROSCIUTTO OR SERRANO HAM	12

BLUE CHEESE DIP: IN A BOWL, STIR TOGETHER MAYONNAISE, CHEESE, OIL, LEMON JUICE AND PEPPER UNTIL COMBINED. SCRAPE INTO A SMALL SERVING DISH; SET ASIDE.

PROSCIUTTO-WRAPPED ASPARAGUS: PREHEAT GRILL TO MEDIUM-HIGH HEAT. SNAP TOUGH ENDS OFF ASPARAGUS AND DISCARD. TOSS ASPARAGUS WITH OIL AND PEPPER.

CUT PROSCIUTTO IN HALF LENGTHWISE AND WRAP EACH HALF AROUND ONE OF THE ASPARAGUS SPEARS. REPEAT WITH REMAINING INGREDIENTS. PLACE ON A GREASED GRILL FOR ABOUT 8 MINUTES, TURNING OCCASIONALLY UNTIL GOLDEN AND CRISP AND ASPARAGUS IS TENDER CRISP. SERVE WITH DIPPING SAUCE. MAKES 24 ASPARAGUS SPEARS OR 6 TO 8 SERVINGS.

TIP: SUBSTITUTE THIN CRISP BREADSTICKS FOR THE ASPARAGUS FOR A NO-GRILLING-REQUIRED OPTION TO DIP INTO THE SAUCE.

TIP: FOR SOMETHING DIFFERENT, TRY WRAPPING CANTALOUPE OR HONEYDEW MELON WITH THE PROSCIUTTO FOR A BEFORE-DINNER APPETIZER — NO NEED FOR GRILLING OR DIPPING SAUCE.

SMOKED SALMON AND RADISH DIP

EMILY'S COUSIN SARAH BROUGHT THIS DIP TO SHARE WITH FRIENDS AND SERVED IT UP WITH EVERYTHING BAGEL SPICED PRETZEL CHIPS. IT WAS A BIG SUCCESS. VEGGIE STICKS OR THICK KETTLE CHIPS WOULD ALSO BE GREAT CRUNCHY DIPPERS.

1 CUP	SMOOTH COTTAGE CHEESE	250 ML
3/4 CUP	SOUR CREAM	175 ML
PINCH	EACH SALT AND BLACK PEPPER	PINCH
4 OZ	SMOKED SALMON, FINELY CHOPPED	125 G
1/2 CUP	FINELY CHOPPED RED RADISHES (ABOUT HALF BUNCH)	125 ML
1	GARLIC CLOVE, MINCED	1

IN A LARGE BOWL, BEAT TOGETHER COTTAGE CHEESE, SOUR CREAM, SALT AND PEPPER. STIR IN SALMON, RADISHES AND GARLIC. TRANSFER TO A SERVING BOWL. MAKES 2 CUPS (500 ML).

MAKE AHEAD: COVER AND REFRIGERATE IN AIRTIGHT CONTAINER FOR UP TO 2 DAYS; LET STAND AT ROOM TEMPERATURE FOR 30 MINUTES BEFORE SERVING.

ROASTED EGGPLANT TOMATO DIP

ROASTING THE VEGETABLES AT A HIGH HEAT BRINGS OUT THE NATURAL SWEETNESS IN THE EGGPLANT AND TOMATOES. SERVE WARM WITH CRUSTY BREAD OR YOUR FAVORITE CRACKERS.

1/2 CUP	EXTRA VIRGIN OLIVE OIL, DIVIDED	125 ML
1	MEDIUM EGGPLANT, PEELED AND CHOPPED (ABOUT 1 LB/500 G)	1
3 CUPS	GRAPE TOMATOES	750 ML
6	LARGE GARLIC CLOVES, SLICED IN HALF	6
1/2 TSP	EACH SALT AND BLACK PEPPER	2 ML
1 1/2 TSP	SMOKED PAPRIKA	7 ML
1/4 CUP	GRATED PARMESAN CHEESE	60 ML

PREHEAT OVEN TO 425°F (220°C). LINE A RIMMED BAKING SHEET WITH PARCHMENT PAPER. PLACE EGGPLANT, TOMATOES AND GARLIC ON PREPARED BAKING SHEET; DRIZZLE WITH 2 TBSP (30 ML) OF THE OIL AND SPRINKLE WITH SALT AND PEPPER. ROAST 35 TO 40 MINUTES OR UNTIL EGGPLANT IS GOLDEN AND TOMATOES ARE TENDER. LET COOL 5 MINUTES.

TRANSFER WARM VEGETABLES TO A FOOD PROCESSOR, THEN ADD SMOKED PAPRIKA. PURÉE, DRIZZLING IN THE REMAINING OIL, UNTIL SMOOTH. TRANSFER TO A BOWL AND STIR IN CHEESE. MAKES 2 CUPS.

TIP: ANY VARIETY OF EGGPLANT WILL WORK WELL IN THIS RECIPE.

SUN-DRIED TOMATO AND ARTICHOKE DIP

A TANGY AND DELICIOUS APPETIZER THAT IS PERFECT FOR ANY GET-TOGETHER. YOU MIGHT WANT TO DOUBLE THE RECIPE AS YOU WILL WANT TO EAT THIS WITH A SPOON! SERVE WITH VEGETABLE STICKS AND CRACKERS.

2 CUPS	CHOPPED MARINATED ARTICHOKES, DRAINED	500 ML
3/4 CUP	PLAIN GREEK-STYLE-STYLE YOGURT OR SOUR CREAM	175 ML
1/3 CUP	FINELY CHOPPED OIL-PACKED SUNDRIED TOMATOES, DRAINED	75 ML
2	GREEN ONIONS, FINELY CHOPPED	2
1 TSP	LEMON JUICE	5 ML
1/2 TSP	EACH SALT AND BLACK PEPPER	2 ML

IN A MEDIUM BOWL, COMBINE ARTICHOKES, YOGURT, TOMATOES, GREEN ONION, LEMON JUICE, SALT AND PEPPER. STORE IN REFRIGERATOR UNTIL READY TO SERVE FOR UP TO 4 DAYS. MAKES 2 CUPS (500 ML).

TIP: LOOK FOR OIL-PACKED SUN-DRIED TOMATOES IN THE CONDIMENT AISLE OF THE GROCERY STORE.

SALADS AND SANDWICHES

ORANGE WHEATBERRY APPLE SALAD

WHEAT BERRIES ARE THE WHOLE GRAINS THAT COME FROM THE WHEAT KERNEL. IN SALADS, THEY ADD A WONDERFUL CHEWY TEXTURE AND ARE A WONDERFUL MATCH WITH FRUIT.

I CUP	WHEAT BERRIES (HARD OR SOFT WHEAT KERNELS)	250 ML
I	ORANGE	I
I	APPLE, CORED AND DICED	I
2 TBSP	CANOLA OIL	30 ML
2 TBSP	CIDER VINEGAR	30 ML
2 TSP	DIJON MUSTARD	IO ML
$\frac{1}{4}$ TSP	EACH SALT AND BLACK PEPPER	I ML

IN LARGE POT OF BOILING WATER, SIMMER WHEAT BERRIES, PARTIALLY COVERED, FOR ABOUT I HOUR OR UNTIL TENDER BUT STILL SLIGHTLY CHEWY. DRAIN AND RINSE UNDER COLD WATER UNTIL COOL. DRAIN WELL AND PLACE IN LARGE BOWL.

USING A RASP, ZEST $\frac{1}{2}$ TSP (2 ML) OF RIND FROM THE ORANGE AND PLACE IN A SMALL BOWL. CUT AWAY SKIN AND PITH FROM ORANGE AND DICE THE FLESH. ADD TO WHEAT BERRIES WITH APPLE.

ADD OIL, VINEGAR, MUSTARD, SALT AND PEPPER TO ORANGE RIND AND WHISK TOGETHER. POUR OVER SALAD AND STIR TO COAT. SERVES 4 TO 6.

BARLEY VARIATION: SUBSTITUTE BARLEY FOR WHEAT BERRIES AND COOK FOR ABOUT 30 MINUTES.

QUINOA VARIATION: SUBSTITUTE RED QUINOA FOR THE WHEAT BERRIES AND COOK FOR ABOUT 15 MINUTES; DRAIN WELL BEFORE USING IN SALAD.

TIP: SALAD CAN BE COVERED AND REFRIGERATED FOR UP TO 2 DAYS.

TIP: COOK WHEAT BERRIES AHEAD AND DRAIN AND LET COOL COMPLETELY. PLACE IN RESEALABLE BAGS AND FREEZE FOR UP TO 3 MONTHS. LET THEM THAW BEFORE USING IN THIS RECIPE.

WHAT PROMPTED THE LAST MASSIVE VEGGIE PROTEST? PRIVILEGED INFORMATION WAS LEEKED.

GRILLED HALOUMI
CORN SALAD

THIS SEMIHARD GRILLING CHEESE MAKES A DELICIOUS SALAD THAT WILL MATCH UP WITH ANY GRILLED PROTEIN. TO ADD CRUNCH TO THIS SALAD, SERVE IT ON CHOPPED ROMAINE LETTUCE.

1	PACKAGE (8 OZ/250 G) HALOUMI CHEESE	1
2	COBS OF CORN, SHUCKED	2
1/4 CUP	EXTRA VIRGIN OLIVE OIL, DIVIDED	60 ML
3 TBSP	BASIL OR SUN-DRIED TOMATO PESTO	45 ML
2 TBSP	AGED BALSAMIC VINEGAR	30 ML
1/4 TSP	EACH SALT AND BLACK PEPPER	1 ML
3	RIPE BUT FIRM TOMATOES, CHOPPED	3

PREHEAT GRILL TO MEDIUM HIGH HEAT. SLICE HALOUMI IN FOUR LENGTHWISE PIECES AND PLACE ON PLATE WITH COBS OF CORN. DRIZZLE BOTH WITH 2 TBSP (30 ML) OF THE OIL. IN A BOWL, WHISK TOGETHER REMAINING OIL, PESTO, VINEGAR, SALT AND PEPPER; SET ASIDE.

GRILL HALOUMI AND CORN OVER MEDIUM-HIGH HEAT ON WELL-GREASED GRILL FOR ABOUT 8 MINUTES OR UNTIL GRILL MARKS APPEAR AND CHEESE IS SOFTENING. RETURN TO PLATE. LET COOL SLIGHTLY.

CUT KERNELS OFF COBS OF CORN AND PLACE IN A LARGE BOWL. CHOP HALOUMI AND ADD TO BOWL WITH TOMATOES. POUR DRESSING OVER TOP AND TOSS GENTLY TO COAT. MAKES 2 TO 3 SERVINGS.

SKILLET VARIATION: HEAT SKILLET OVER MEDIUM-HIGH HEAT AND BROWN CORN COBS THEN REMOVE AND PAN-FRY HALOUMI ON BOTH SIDES.

TIP: SEE THE BASIL PESTO RECIPE ON PAGE 206 TO MAKE YOUR OWN.

MAKE AHEAD: YOU CAN MAKE THIS SALAD AHEAD OF TIME AND ENJOY LATER. COVER AND REFRIGERATE FOR UP TO 1 DAY.

HALOUMI-TOPPED SALAD GREENS

HALOUMI IS A MIDDLE EASTERN SEMIHARD, UNRIPENED BRINED CHEESE. WHEN SEARED, THIS CHEESE SOFTENS, BROWNS EASILY AND HOLDS ITS SHAPE.

6 OZ	HALOUMI CHEESE, SLICED $\frac{1}{2}$ INCH (1 CM) THICK	175 G
3 TBSP	CANOLA OIL, DIVIDED	45 ML
6 CUPS	MIXED SALAD GREENS	1.5 L
2 CUPS	SLICED GRAPE TOMATOES	500 ML
$\frac{1}{4}$ CUP	BASIL PESTO	60 ML
1 TBSP	LEMON JUICE	15 ML

IN A NONSTICK SKILLET, HEAT 1 TBSP (15 ML) OIL OVER MEDIUM-HIGH HEAT, PANFRY HALOUMI SLICES FOR ABOUT 30 TO 60 SECONDS PER SIDE, UNTIL GOLDEN BROWN. COOL SLIGHTLY, THEN CUT INTO CUBES. DIVIDE SALAD GREENS, TOMATOES AND CHEESE ONTO FOUR PLATES. IN A SMALL BOWL, COMBINE PESTO, LEMON JUICE AND REMAINING 2 TBSP (30 ML) OIL. DRIZZLE DRESSING OVER SALAD. SERVES 4.

TIP: SEE OUR BASIL PESTO RECIPE ON PAGE 206 TO MAKE YOUR OWN.

TIP: SALAD GREENS TEND TO STAY FRESHER FOR LONGER IF STORED IN A LOOSELY COVERED CONTAINER, ALONG WITH A PAPER TOWEL OR TEA TOWEL TO ABSORB EXCESS MOISTURE BUILDUP.

BAT SALAD

YOU WILL HIT A HOME RUN WITH THIS SALAD, AND YOU WON'T NEED A BAT TO MAKE IT! THIS BAT STANDS FOR BACON, ARUGULA AND TOMATO: A MIX THAT COMBINES THE CRISPY CRUNCH OF BACON WITH A PEPPERY BITE OF ARUGULA AND THE JUICINESS OF TOMATOES. IT'S A PERFECT SALAD TO ENJOY ANY TIME OF THE DAY!

1	PACKAGE (12 OZ/375 G) SLICED BACON	1
1	PACKAGE (5 OZ/142 G) BABY ARUGULA	1
2	RIPE BUT FIRM TOMATOES, CUT INTO WEDGES	2
1 CUP	SEASONED CROUTONS	250 ML
3 TBSP	CANOLA OIL	45 ML
3 TBSP	CIDER VINEGAR	45 ML
1/2 TSP	SALT	2 ML
1/4 TSP	BLACK PEPPER	1 ML

PREHEAT OVEN TO 400°F (200°C). LINE A BAKING SHEET WITH FOIL. PLACE BACON SLICES IN SINGLE LAYER ON BAKING SHEET. BAKE FOR ABOUT 15 MINUTES OR UNTIL CRISPY. REMOVE TO PAPER TOWEL-LINED PLATE TO DRAIN. CHOP BACON.

MEANWHILE IN A LARGE SHALLOW BOWL OR PLATTER, SPREAD OUT THE ARUGULA AND TOP WITH TOMATOES AND CROUTONS. IN A SMALL BOWL, WHISK TOGETHER OIL, VINEGAR, SALT AND PEPPER. POUR OVER SALAD. CRUMBLE BACON OVER TOP AND TOSS GENTLY TO SERVE. SERVES 4.

POTATO, BEAN AND TOMATO SALAD

THIS CREAMY SPIN ON POTATO SALAD IS A PERFECT ADDITION TO A VEGETARIAN MENU.

4	YELLOW-FLESHED POTATOES, PEELED	4
1/4 CUP	MAYONNAISE	60 ML
2 TBSP	EXTRA VIRGIN OLIVE OIL	30 ML
3/4 TSP	SALT	3 ML
1/2 TSP	BLACK PEPPER	2 ML
2	RIPE BUT FIRM TOMATOES, CHOPPED	2
1	CAN (19 OZ/540 ML) ROMANO OR RED KIDNEY BEANS, DRAINED AND RINSED	1
1/3 CUP	THINLY SLICED RED ONION	75 ML

CUT POTATOES INTO 2-INCH (5 CM) CHUNKS. BRING POT OF WATER AND POTATOES TO BOIL FOR ABOUT 15 MINUTES OR UNTIL TENDER BUT FIRM. DRAIN WELL AND PLACE IN LARGE BOWL; LET COOL SLIGHTLY.

MEANWHILE, IN ANOTHER SMALL BOWL, WHISK TOGETHER MAYONNAISE, OIL, SALT AND PEPPER. POUR OVER POTATO MIXTURE AND TOSS GENTLY TO COMBINE. STIR IN TOMATOES, BEANS AND ONION GENTLY TO COAT. SERVES 2 TO 4.

TIP: THIS IS A GREAT WAY TO USE UP LEFTOVER ROASTED OR GRILLED POTATOES.

TIP: USE YOUR FAVORITE TYPE OF CANNED BEANS IN THE RECIPE.

TIP: NO TOMATOES? NO PROBLEM. ADD A CAN OF TUNA TO THE MIX INSTEAD. OR FOR SOMETHING CRUNCHY, ADD A CHOPPED GREEN OR RED BELL PEPPER.

ROASTED CORN
AND BACON SALAD

*SCORCHING THE CORN ADDS A SMOKY NOTE
TO THIS FRESH SALAD. THE SILKY GUACAMOLE
DOUBLES AS A DRESSING AND FLAVOR BOOSTER.
ONCE SALAD IS ASSEMBLED, SERVE RIGHT
AWAY, AS THE AVOCADO WILL DISCOLOR.*

2 TBSP	CANOLA OIL	30 ML
3 CUPS	FROZEN CORN, THAWED AND DRAINED	375 ML
I	RED BELL PEPPER, DICED	I
2	GREEN ONIONS, FINELY CHOPPED	2
I CUP	GUACAMOLE	250 ML
	SALT AND BLACK PEPPER	
8	CRISP COOKED BACON SLICES, CHOPPED	8

IN A SKILLET, HEAT OIL OVER MEDIUM-HIGH HEAT.
ADD CORN AND COOK FOR ABOUT 7 MINUTES, STIRRING
OCCASIONALLY, UNTIL CORN BEGINS TO BROWN AND
SCORCH SLIGHTLY. REMOVE FROM HEAT AND TRANSFER
TO A LARGE BOWL TO COOL COMPLETELY. STIR IN RED
PEPPER, ONIONS AND GUACAMOLE UNTIL WELL COMBINED.
SEASON WITH SALT AND PEPPER TO TASTE. SPRINKLE
WITH BACON. SERVES 6.

TIP: YOU CAN USE FRESH CORN IF IT IS IN SEASON.

CRAB AVOCADO SALAD

IN THIS RECIPE, THE AVOCADO ACTS LIKE A SALAD BOWL. FOR A VARIATION, YOU CAN SUBSTITUTE THE CILANTRO WITH THE SAME AMOUNT OF CHOPPED GREEN ONION.

I	LEMON	I
I	CAN (6 OZ/170 G) CRABMEAT, WELL DRAINED	I
1/2 CUP	GRAPE TOMATOES, SLICED IN HALF	125 ML
2 TBSP	CHOPPED FRESH CILANTRO	30 ML
I TBSP	EXTRA VIRGIN OLIVE OIL	15 ML
1/4 TSP	EACH SALT AND BLACK PEPPER	I ML
I	LARGE AVOCADO	I

REMOVE I TSP (5 ML) ZEST AND I TBSP (15 ML) JUICE FROM LEMON. PLACE ZEST AND JUICE IN A MEDIUM BOWL. ADD CRAB, TOMATOES, CILANTRO, OIL, SALT AND PEPPER; TOSS GENTLY TO COMBINE. SLICE AVOCADO IN HALF AND REMOVE PIT. MOUND CRAB SALAD ON TOP OF EACH AVOCADO HALF. SERVE WITH LEMON WEDGES ON THE SIDE. SERVES 2.

TIP: AN AVOCADO IS READY TO EAT WHEN IT YIELDS TO FIRM PRESSURE. IT SHOULD FEEL SLIGHTLY SOFT BUT NOT MUSHY.

THAI CHICKEN SALAD

*ENJOY THIS SIMPLE, FRESH AND CRUNCHY
SALAD THAT GETS PLENTY OF FLAVOR
FROM GROCERY STORE CONVENIENCES.*

1/2 CUP	PREPARED SUNDRIED TOMATO SALAD DRESSING	125 ML
1/3 CUP	CRUNCHY PEANUT BUTTER	75 ML
1/2 TSP	BLACK PEPPER	2 ML
2 CUPS	COOKED CHOPPED CHICKEN	500 ML
6 CUPS	COLESLAW MIX	1.5 L
1 CUP	LIGHTLY PACKED CHOPPED CILANTRO	250 ML

IN A LARGE BOWL, COMBINE SALAD DRESSING, PEANUT BUTTER AND PEPPER. ADD CHICKEN, COLESLAW AND CILANTRO; TOSS TO EVENLY COAT. SERVES 6.

TIP: USE THE CILANTRO STEMS AS WELL AS THE LEAVES FOR TEXTURE AND FLAVOR.

TIP: THE CHICKEN CAN BE SHREDDED, SLICED OR CUBED.

SPINACH POCKETS

LITTLE PIZZA POCKETS FILLED WITH A GREEK-INSPIRED MIXTURE ARE SURE TO BE ENJOYED. TRY THEM AS A BUSY ON-THE-GO SANDWICH FOR LUNCH OR AN AFTER-SCHOOL SNACK.

1½ LBS	PIZZA DOUGH	750 G
1	PACKAGE (10 TO 16 OZ/300 TO 500 G) FROZEN CHOPPED SPINACH, THAWED	1
8 OZ	FETA CHEESE, CRUMBLED	250 G
3	LARGE EGGS	3
¼ CUP	EXTRA VIRGIN OLIVE OIL, DIVIDED	60 ML
2	GARLIC CLOVES, MINCED	2
¼ TSP	BLACK PEPPER	1 ML

LET PIZZA DOUGH COME TO ROOM TEMPERATURE AND DIVIDE INTO EIGHT PIECES; SET ASIDE.

MEANWHILE, DRAIN SPINACH AND SQUEEZE DRY. PLACE IN A LARGE BOWL AND ADD FETA, EGGS, 2 TBSP (30 ML) OF THE OIL, GARLIC AND PEPPER. USING YOUR HANDS, MIX WELL TO COMBINE.

PREHEAT OVEN TO 375°F (190°C).

ON A LIGHTLY FLOURED SURFACE, ROLL EACH PIECE OF DOUGH INTO A 6-INCH (15 CM) CIRCLE. DIVIDE FILLING IN CENTER OF EACH PIECE. FOLD OVER AND PINCH SEAM TO SEAL. PLACE ON PARCHMENT PAPER-LINED BAKING SHEET AND BRUSH WITH REMAINING OIL. USING A FORK, PRICK TOP OF POCKET AND BAKE FOR ABOUT 25 MINUTES OR UNTIL GOLDEN BROWN. LET COOL SLIGHTLY BEFORE SERVING. SERVES 6.

TIP: THESE ARE DELICIOUS WITH WHOLE WHEAT PIZZA DOUGH.

BROCCOLI MELTS

GARLICKY BROCCOLI UNDER A BLANKET OF MELTY CHEESE MAKES A GREAT SANDWICH. HAVARTI CHEESE IS A TASTY OPTION TO USE IN THIS RECIPE.

1 LB	BROCCOLI CROWNS, TRIMMED AND CUT INTO FLORETS	500 G
3 TBSP	EXTRA VIRGIN OLIVE OIL, DIVIDED	45 ML
2	GARLIC CLOVES, FINELY CHOPPED	2
	SALT AND BLACK PEPPER	
3 CUPS	SHREDDED JALAPEÑO MONTEREY JACK CHEESE	750 ML
6	LARGE SLICES SOURDOUGH BREAD	6

IN A LARGE POT OF BOILING SALTED WATER, COOK BROCCOLI FOR 2 TO 3 MINUTES, UNTIL SLIGHTLY TENDER. DRAIN WELL AND PAT DRY. IN A MEDIUM SKILLET, HEAT 2 TBSP (30 ML) OIL OVER MEDIUM HEAT; ADD GARLIC AND COOK 30 SECONDS. ADD BROCCOLI AND COOK 2 TO 3 MINUTES, STIRRING UNTIL BROCCOLI IS TENDER CRISP, WATCHING TO MAKE SURE GARLIC DOES NOT BURN. REMOVE FROM HEAT AND SEASON WITH SALT AND PEPPER TO TASTE.

MEANWHILE, PREHEAT BROILER. ON A BAKING SHEET, DRIZZLE REMAINING 1 TBSP (15 ML) OLIVE OIL OVER BREAD SLICES. PLACE IN OVEN AND BROIL UNTIL LIGHTLY TOASTED. REMOVE FROM OVEN AND EVENLY DIVIDE BROCCOLI MIXTURE ONTO EACH SLICE. EVENLY SPRINKLE CHEESE OVER TOP. BROIL ABOUT 1 MINUTE OR UNTIL CHEESE IS MELTED AND GOLDEN. SERVES 6.

TIP: YOU CAN SUBSTITUTE THE SOURDOUGH WITH LARGE SLICES OF MULTIGRAIN BREAD.

TIP: FOR VARIETY, SWITCH OUT THE MONTEREY JACK CHEESE WITH SHARP (AGED) CHEDDAR CHEESE.

TOASTED HAM AND CHEESE CROISSANT SANDWICHES

HOT, CRISPY AND CHEESY DESCRIBE THESE SANDWICHES. THEY'RE EASY TO MAKE AND PERFECT FOR BREAKFAST, LUNCH OR DINNER. DOUBLE THE RECIPE IF YOU'RE FEEDING A CROWD.

6	LARGE CROISSANTS, HALVED HORIZONTALLY	6
$1/4$ CUP	HONEY DIJON MUSTARD	60 ML
12	THIN SLICES SMOKED DELI HAM (ABOUT 12 OZ/375 G)	12
12	SLICES MOZZARELLA OR SWISS CHEESE (ABOUT 12 OZ/375 G)	12
$1\frac{1}{2}$ CUPS	LOOSELY PACKED ARUGULA	375 ML
	BLACK PEPPER	

PREHEAT OVEN TO 350°F (180°C). ON A PARCHMENT-LINED BAKING SHEET, ARRANGE THE BOTTOM HALF OF CROISSANTS IN A SINGLE LAYER. EVENLY DIVIDE HONEY MUSTARD, HAM, CHEESE AND ARUGULA ON CROISSANTS, THEN SPRINKLE WITH PEPPER. COVER WITH THE OTHER HALF OF THE CROISSANTS. BAKE FOR ABOUT 10 TO 12 MINUTES OR UNTIL CHEESE IS MELTY AND CROISSANTS ARE TOASTY AND CRISP ON TOP. SERVES 6.

TIP: SANDWICHES CAN BE ASSEMBLED UP TO 2 DAYS IN ADVANCE. STORE IN A COVERED CONTAINER IN THE FRIDGE. WHEN READY TO EAT, TRANSFER TO BAKING SHEET AND BAKE AS DIRECTED.

CHICKEN MEATBALL FETA WRAPS

USING CONVENIENT, READY-MADE CHICKEN MEATBALLS GETS THIS SANDWICH ON THE TABLE IN A FLASH. ALTERNATIVELY, YOU CAN MAKE OUR EASY HOMEMADE RECIPE FOR CHICKEN MEATBALLS (SEE PAGE 204).

6	GARLIC NAAN	6
1 LB	CHICKEN MEATBALLS, HEATED	500 G
3 CUPS	LOOSELY TORN SPINACH OR ARUGULA	750 ML
3/4 CUP	CUBED FETA CHEESE	175 ML
6 TBSP	PREPARED SUN-DRIED TOMATO SALAD DRESSING	90 ML

HEAT NAAN IN A SKILLET OR MICROWAVE FOR A FEW MINUTES TO WARM THEM UP AND TO HELP MAKE THEM PLIABLE. PLACE EACH NAAN ON A PLATE; EVENLY DIVIDE MEATBALLS, SPINACH AND CHEESE ON TOP, THEN DRIZZLE WITH DRESSING. SERVES 6.

TIP: STORE NAAN AT ROOM TEMPERATURE FOR UP TO 3 DAYS OR FREEZE IN AN AIRTIGHT CONTAINER FOR UP TO 2 MONTHS.

TIP: GARLIC NAAN GIVES GREAT FLAVOR TO THIS SANDWICH. IF YOU ARE UNABLE TO FIND IT, USE GREEK-STYLE PITA. COMPARED TO REGULAR PITA, GREEK PITA IS POCKET-LESS AND IS SOFTER AND THICKER.

MEATBALL SUBS

NO NEED TO GRAB A SUB WHILE YOU'RE OUT WHEN YOU CAN MAKE A DELICIOUS AND MEATY ONE RIGHT AT HOME! KEEP THE MEATBALLS IN THE FREEZER SO YOU CAN WARM THEM UP IN THE SAUCE FOR ADDED FLAVOR.

1 TBSP	CANOLA OIL	15 ML
8 OZ	BUTTON MUSHROOMS, SLICED	250 G
1/2 TSP	EACH SALT AND BLACK PEPPER	2 ML
16	COOKED BEEF MEATBALLS (SEE PAGE 205)	16
3 CUPS	PASTA SAUCE (SEE PAGE 207)	750 ML
4	ITALIAN SUB BUNS, SPLIT	4
1 1/3 CUPS	SHREDDED ITALIAN BLEND CHEESE	325 ML

IN A LARGE NONSTICK SKILLET, HEAT OIL OVER MEDIUM-HIGH HEAT. ADD MUSHROOMS, SALT AND PEPPER AND SAUTÉ ABOUT 8 MINUTES OR UNTIL STARTING TO BROWN. ADD MEATBALLS AND TOMATO SAUCE; BRING TO A SIMMER; COVER AND COOK FOR ABOUT 10 MINUTES OR UNTIL MEATBALLS ARE HOT THROUGHOUT.

TOAST BUNS, IF DESIRED. SPRINKLE HALF OF THE CHEESE ON BOTTOM OF EACH BUN AND DIVIDE MEATBALLS AND SAUCE AMONG BUNS. TOP WITH REMAINING CHEESE. SERVES 4.

SOUPS

CHICKEN MEATBALL VEGGIE SOUP

A WARM AND SATISFYING SOUP IS WELCOME AT ANY TABLE. OUR HOMEMADE CHICKEN MEATBALLS (SEE PAGE 204) ARE DELICIOUS IN THIS ONE. IF YOU'RE IN A HURRY AND HAVE STORE-BOUGHT MEATBALLS IN THE FREEZER, THEN USE THEM INSTEAD. ADD THEM STRAIGHT TO THE POT AND SIMMER A FEW MINUTES LONGER TO MAKE SURE THEY'RE HEATED THROUGH.

8 CUPS	READY-TO-USE CHICKEN BROTH	2 L
4 CUPS	FROZEN MIXED VEGETABLES	1 L
1 LB	COOKED CHICKEN MEATBALLS	500 G
3 CUPS	SPINACH, COARSELY CHOPPED	750 ML
1/4 CUP	GRATED PARMESAN CHEESE	60 ML
	SALT AND BLACK PEPPER	

IN A LARGE POT, OVER MEDIUM-HIGH HEAT, BRING CHICKEN STOCK TO A BOIL. ADD MIXED VEGETABLES AND MEATBALLS; COVER AND BRING TO A BOIL, THEN REDUCE HEAT TO MEDIUM AND SIMMER 8 TO 10 MINUTES OR UNTIL HEATED THROUGH. STIR IN SPINACH, THEN COVER POT. TURN OFF HEAT AND LET SIT 5 MINUTES, UNTIL SPINACH IS WILTED. SEASON WITH SALT AND PEPPER, TO TASTE. LADLE INTO BOWLS AND SPRINKLE WITH CHEESE. SERVES 6.

TIP: FOR A FLAVOR VARIATION, USE ARUGULA INSTEAD OF SPINACH.

Blender Banana Oatmeal Pancakes (page 10)

Baked Egg Bites (page 13)

James's Sausage-Stuffed Jalapeño Peppers (page 28)

Fig Jam and Goat Cheese Tart (page 30)

Sun-Dried Tomato and Artichoke Dip (page 44)

BAT Salad (page 51)

Thai Chicken Salad (page 55)

Spinach Pockets (page 56)

SOUTHWESTERN BEEF MEATBALL SOUP

*YOU CAN HAVE HEARTY BOWLS OF HOT SOUP
READY IN MINUTES. TEX-MEX CHEESE BLEND
IS USUALLY A COMBINATION OF CHEDDAR AND
MONTEREY JACK WITH JALAPEÑO, BUT ANY
COMBINATION OF CHEESE WILL WORK WELL.*

4 CUPS	READY-TO-USE CHICKEN BROTH	1 L
1¼ CUPS	SALSA	300 ML
1 LB	COOKED BEEF MEATBALLS	500 G
1	CAN (19 OZ/540 ML) MIXED BEANS, DRAINED AND RINSED (2 CUPS/500 ML)	1
1 CUP	TEX-MEX SHREDDED CHEESE BLEND	250 ML

IN A LARGE POT, OVER MEDIUM-HIGH HEAT, BRING CHICKEN
STOCK AND SALSA TO A BOIL. ADD MEATBALLS AND BEANS,
COVER AND COOK 8 TO 10 MINUTES, OR UNTIL HEATED
THROUGH. LADLE INTO BOWLS AND SPRINKLE CHEESE
OVER TOP. SERVES 4.

TIP: YOU CAN PURCHASE PREPARED BEEF MEATBALLS OR
CAN MAKE YOUR OWN USING OUR BEEF MEATBALLS RECIPE
ON PAGE 205.

MADRAS CURRY CHICKEN SOUP

WE LOVE ALL KINDS OF CURRY, SO WE KNEW THAT MAKING CURRIED SOUP FINISHED WITH COCONUT MILK WOULD BE A FAMILY FAVORITE. COMPARED TO COMMON CURRY PASTE, THE MADRAS CURRY IS USUALLY HOTTER IN FLAVOR AND DARKER IN COLOR, AS IT HAS MORE RED CHILIES. USE WHATEVER CURRY YOU HAVE ON HAND AND ADD ADDITIONAL HOT SAUCE OR GROUND CHILIES FOR MORE HEAT. SERVE WITH NAAN AND FRESH CHOPPED CILANTRO, IF DESIRED.

1 TBSP	CANOLA OIL	15 ML
6	BONELESS, SKINLESS CHICKEN THIGHS, CUT INTO $3/4$-INCH (2 CM) CUBES	6
1	ONION, FINELY DICED	1
3 TBSP	MADRAS CURRY PASTE	45 ML
2 CUPS	WATER	500 ML
2 CUPS	PASTA SAUCE (SEE PAGE 207)	500 ML
$3/4$ CUP	COCONUT MILK	175 ML
	SALT AND BLACK PEPPER	

IN A LARGE POT, HEAT OIL OVER MEDIUM-HIGH HEAT. ADD CHICKEN AND ONION AND SAUTÉ 8 MINUTES, STIRRING ONCE OR TWICE. STIR IN CURRY PASTE; COOK 30 SECONDS. ADD WATER AND SCRAPE UP ANY BROWNED FLAVOR BITS IN THE BOTTOM OF THE POT, THEN STIR IN PASTA SAUCE. BRING TO A BOIL; REDUCE HEAT TO MEDIUM AND LET SIMMER, UNCOVERED, FOR 15 MINUTES. STIR IN COCONUT MILK AND ADD SALT AND PEPPER, TO TASTE. SERVES 6.

TIP: BE SURE TO USE CURRY PASTE AND NOT CURRY SAUCE. THE PASTE IS MORE CONCENTRATED IN FLAVOR.

TOMATO RAVIOLI SOUP

LOOK FOR MINI RAVIOLI IN THE FREEZER AND
FRESH PASTA SECTIONS OF YOUR GROCERY
STORE. IF THEY ARE UNAVAILABLE, YOU CAN USE
SMALLER SIZED RAVIOLI INSTEAD. EITHER WAY,
THEY MAKE THIS SOUP DIFFERENT THAN THE REST.

1 LB	FRESH OR FROZEN MEAT OR CHEESE RAVIOLI	500 G
2 TBSP	CANOLA OIL	30 ML
1	ONION, DICED	1
4	GARLIC CLOVES, MINCED	4
1	JAR (2$\frac{3}{4}$ CUPS/700 ML) TOMATO BASIL PASTA SAUCE, OR SEE PASTA SAUCE (PAGE 207)	1
2 CUPS	WATER	500 ML
$\frac{1}{4}$ TSP	EACH SALT AND BLACK PEPPER	1 ML
1	PACKAGE (5 OZ/142 G) BABY SPINACH	1

IN LARGE POT OF BOILING SALTED WATER, COOK RAVIOLI
FOR 5 MINUTES OR UNTIL THEY FLOAT TO THE TOP.
DRAIN; SET ASIDE.

MEANWHILE, IN A LARGE SAUCEPAN, HEAT OIL OVER
MEDIUM HEAT. ADD ONION AND GARLIC AND COOK FOR
5 MINUTES OR UNTIL SOFTENED AND STARTING TO
BROWN. ADD PASTA SAUCE, WATER, SALT AND PEPPER;
BRING TO A BOIL. STIR IN RAVIOLI AND SPINACH; SIMMER
FOR 5 MINUTES. SERVES 4.

TORTELLINI VARIATION: SUBSTITUTE TORTELLINI FOR
THE RAVIOLI.

LEMONGRASS SHRIMP SOUP

THIS IS A FLAVORFUL, LIGHT BROTH-BASED SOUP. ON DAYS WHEN YOU FEEL YOU WANT SOMETHING A BIT MORE HEARTY, SERVE THIS WITH COOKED RICE NOODLES.

1 LB	LARGE SHELL-ON SHRIMP	500 G
4	LEMONGRASS STALKS, WHITE PART	4
6 CUPS	READY-TO-USE CHICKEN BROTH	1.5 L
1 TBSP	SLIVERED FRESH GINGER	15 ML
1 TSP	SRIRACHA	5 ML

SHELL AND DEVEIN THE SHRIMP, THEN PLACE THE SHELLS AND TAILS IN A MEDIUM SAUCEPAN. SET ASIDE SHRIMP. WITH THE BACK OF A KNIFE OR A KITCHEN MALLET, BASH THE LEMONGRASS STALKS TO RELEASE THE FLAVOR, THEN SLICE IN HALF LENGTHWISE. TO THE SAUCEPAN, ADD LEMONGRASS, CHICKEN BROTH, GINGER AND SRIRACHA.

OVER MEDIUM-HIGH HEAT, BRING TO A BOIL, THEN COVER AND REDUCE HEAT TO MEDIUM AND SIMMER FOR 20 MINUTES. DISCARD SHRIMP SHELLS AND LEMONGRASS, LEAVING GINGER. ADD SHRIMP AND COOK 1 TO 2 MINUTES, OR UNTIL PINK AND OPAQUE. SERVES 4.

TIP: SHRIMP ARE SOLD BY COUNT PER POUND. THE HIGHER THE NUMBER, THE SMALLER THE SHRIMP. LARGE SHRIMP IS LABELED 31/35, MEANING THERE ARE 31 TO 35 SHRIMP IN EACH POUND.

CHUNKY CHICKEN MINESTRONE

USE A ROTISSERIE CHICKEN AND CREATE A NEW DINNER FOR YOUR FAMILY. FULL OF CHICKEN, BEANS AND GREENS, THIS IS A HEARTY BOWL OF SOUP THAT WILL WARM YOUR TUMMY AND YOUR HEART DURING A BUSY WEEK. THERE WILL BE ENOUGH FOR LEFTOVERS FOR LUNCH TO TOTE TO WORK TOO!

1	ROTISSERIE CHICKEN (ABOUT 2 LBS/1 KG)	1
1	CAN (28 OZ/796 ML) CHUNKY OR DICED TOMATOES WITH BASIL	1
1	CAN (19 OZ/540 ML) MIXED BEANS, DRAINED AND RINSED	1
4 CUPS	WATER	1 L
3 CUPS	FROZEN MIXED GREENS OR VEGETABLES	750 ML
1/2 CUP	SMALL PASTA, SUCH AS BABY SHELLS OR TUBETTI/DITALI	125 ML
1/4 TSP	EACH SALT AND BLACK PEPPER	1 ML

REMOVE MEAT FROM CHICKEN AND CHOP COARSELY. DISCARD BONES AND SKIN OF CHICKEN. PLACE MEAT IN A LARGE SOUP POT. ADD TOMATOES, BEANS AND WATER. BRING TO A BOIL.

ADD GREENS AND PASTA AND SIMMER FOR ABOUT 10 MINUTES, OR UNTIL PASTA IS TENDER AND FLAVORS HAVE DEVELOPED. SERVES 8.

TIP: IF THERE ARE LEFTOVERS OF THE SOUP, BE SURE TO STIR IN SOME MORE WATER, AS THE PASTA TENDS TO ABSORB THE LIQUID AS IT SITS.

CORN CHOWDER

YOU CAN PUT TOGETHER A SIMPLE SOUP
LIKE THIS IN MINUTES WITH A FEW PANTRY
STAPLES. IF YOU HAPPEN TO HAVE SOME HOT
SAUCE ON HAND, ADD A FEW DASHES INTO
YOUR BOWL — IT WILL SURELY WARM YOUR HEART.

1 LB	YELLOW-FLESHED POTATOES (ABOUT 4), PEELED AND DICED	500 G
1 CUP	WATER	250 ML
1 1/2 CUPS	VEGETABLE BROTH	375 ML
1	CAN (14 OZ/398 ML) CREAMED CORN	1
1	CAN (12 OZ OR 370 ML) 2% EVAPORATED MILK	1
2 TSP	OLD BAY SEASONING	10 ML
	BLACK PEPPER	

IN A SAUCEPAN, COVER POTATOES WITH WATER AND
BRING TO A SIMMER. COVER AND COOK FOR 5 MINUTES.
REMOVE LID AND ADD BROTH, CREAMED CORN,
EVAPORATED MILK AND SEASONING.

USE POTATO MASHER TO MASH SLIGHTLY, THEN
RETURN TO A SIMMER. SIMMER FOR ABOUT 15 MINUTES
OR UNTIL POTATOES ARE VERY SOFT AND FLAVORS
COME TOGETHER. SEASON WITH PEPPER, IF DESIRED.
SERVES 3 TO 4.

SIMPLE SPLIT PEA SOUP

A HUMBLE SOUP THAT OFFERS CLASSIC
COMFORT. IF THE DRIED PEAS ARE VERY
OLD, THEY MAY TAKE LONGER TO COOK.

3 TBSP	CANOLA OIL	45 ML
2	ONIONS, FINELY CHOPPED	2
4	CARROTS, DICED	4
3 CUPS	DRIED YELLOW SPLIT PEAS, RINSED AND DRAINED	750 ML
8 OZ	CUBED SMOKED HAM (ABOUT 1½ CUPS/375 ML)	250 G
8 CUPS	CHICKEN STOCK	2 L
	BLACK PEPPER	

IN A LARGE POT, HEAT OIL OVER MEDIUM-HIGH HEAT.
SAUTÉ ONION FOR ABOUT 8 MINUTES, STIRRING
OCCASIONALLY, UNTIL LIGHT GOLDEN BROWN. ADD
CARROTS, PEAS, HAM AND STOCK; BRING TO A BOIL.
REDUCE HEAT TO LOW, COVER AND SIMMER FOR
1½ HOURS, UNTIL SPLIT PEAS ARE CREAMY AND SOFT.
STIR OCCASIONALLY AND ADD MORE BROTH OR WATER
IF SOUP IS TOO THICK. SEASON WITH PEPPER TO TASTE.
SERVES 8 TO 10.

TIP: THIS SOUP KEEPS WELL IN THE REFRIGERATOR FOR
UP TO 3 DAYS.

CHILLED TOMATO SOUP

A PERFECTLY REFRESHING SOUP WHEN THE WEATHER IS HOT AND FLAVORFUL TOMATOES ARE IN SEASON. THIS SOUP IS A GREAT MAKE-AHEAD AND REQUIRES ONLY A FEW MINUTES TO PREPARE.

2	TOMATOES, CHOPPED	2
1/2	ENGLISH CUCUMBER, CHOPPED	1/2
1	GREEN ONION, FINELY CHOPPED	1
4 CUPS	SPICY TOMATO CLAM COCKTAIL	1 L
1 TSP	BALSAMIC VINEGAR	5 ML
1/2 TSP	EACH SALT AND BLACK PEPPER	2 ML
	EXTRA VIRGIN OLIVE OIL FOR DRIZZLING	

IN A FOOD PROCESSOR OR BLENDER, COMBINE TOMATOES, CUCUMBER AND ONION. PULSE UNTIL FINELY CHOPPED, BUT NOT PURÉED, SO THE SOUP HAS A BIT OF TEXTURE. ADD TOMATO CLAM COCKTAIL, VINEGAR, SALT AND PEPPER AND PULSE ONCE OR TWICE TO JUST COMBINE INGREDIENTS. PLACE BLENDER JAR IN REFRIGERATOR. IF USING A FOOD PROCESSOR, TRANSFER SOUP TO A PITCHER OR A LARGE BOWL AND COVER. REFRIGERATE FOR AT LEAST 1 HOUR BEFORE SERVING.

WHEN READY TO SERVE, GIVE SOUP A STIR TO REDISTRIBUTE INGREDIENTS THEN DIVIDE INTO FOUR BOWLS. TOP EACH WITH A GENEROUS DRIZZLE OF OLIVE OIL. SERVES 4.

TIP: THIS SOUP IMPROVES WITH TIME AND CAN BE MADE THE NIGHT BEFORE.

TIP: FEEL FREE TO GARNISH WITH CROUTONS, SOUR CREAM, CUCUMBER SLICES, DICED AVOCADO, HOT PEPPER SAUCE OR CHOPPED FRESH HERBS, SUCH AS CILANTRO, PARSLEY OR DILL.

TIP: IF ENGLISH CUCUMBERS ARE NOT AVAILABLE, USE A WHOLE REGULAR CUCUMBER. BE SURE TO REMOVE THE THICKER SKIN AND SEEDS WITH THIS SUBSTITUTION.

EVERYTHING MAKES BROTH.
—ITALIAN PROVERB

PIZZA SOUP

ENJOY THE FLAVORS OF PIZZA IN A BOWL INSTEAD OF A SLICE! GET THE KIDS TO HELP WITH THIS ONE AND WATCH HOW THEIR EYES LIGHT UP AS THEY SEE HOW QUICKLY IT COMES TOGETHER.

12 OZ	PIZZA DOUGH	375 G
3 TBSP	CANOLA OIL, DIVIDED	45 ML
1¼ CUPS	SHREDDED MOZZARELLA CHEESE, DIVIDED	300 ML
1	SMALL ONION, CHOPPED	1
1 CUP	CHOPPED SLICED PEPPERONI	250 ML
1½ CUPS	PIZZA SAUCE	375 ML
2½ CUPS	WATER	625 ML

PREHEAT OVEN TO 400°F (200°C). ON A FLOURED WORK SURFACE, ROLL OUT PIZZA DOUGH TO A 10- BY 8-INCH (25 BY 20 CM) RECTANGLE. CUT INTO 12 THICK STRIPS AND PLACE ON PARCHMENT PAPER-LINED BAKING SHEET. BRUSH WITH 1 TBSP (15 ML) OF THE OIL. SPRINKLE WITH ⅓ CUP (75 ML) OF THE CHEESE. BAKE FOR ABOUT 12 MINUTES OR UNTIL GOLDEN BROWN; SET ASIDE.

MEANWHILE, IN A SAUCEPAN, HEAT REMAINING OIL OVER MEDIUM HEAT AND SAUTÉ ONION FOR 3 MINUTES OR UNTIL SOFTENED. ADD PEPPERONI AND COOK FOR 4 MINUTES OR UNTIL STARTING TO BROWN. POUR IN WATER AND PIZZA SAUCE; BRING TO A BOIL. REDUCE HEAT TO A SIMMER AND COOK FOR 10 MINUTES. LADLE INTO BOWLS AND TOP EACH WITH REMAINING CHEESE. SERVE WITH PIZZA BREADSTICKS IN EACH BOWL. SERVES 3 TO 4.

BEEF AND VEAL

GRILLED FLANK STEAK
WITH BRUSCHETTA TOPPING

STEAK ON THE GRILL IS A SURE SIGN OF SUMMER,
BUT YOU CAN EASILY ENJOY IT YEAR ROUND!
FOR A JUICY TENDER STEAK, GRILL FLANK
STEAK OUTSIDE, ON THE BARBECUE, OR INSIDE,
IN A GRILL PAN OR UNDER THE BROILER.

1	FLANK, TRI-TIP OR SKIRT STEAK, ABOUT 1$\frac{1}{2}$ LBS (750 G)	1
2 TBSP	CANOLA OIL	30 ML
2 TBSP	BALSAMIC VINEGAR	30 ML
2 TBSP	SOY SAUCE	30 ML
2	GARLIC CLOVES, MINCED	2
$\frac{1}{2}$ TSP	BLACK PEPPER	2 ML
	SALT	
1 CUP	PREPARED BRUSCHETTA TOPPING	250 ML

PLACE FLANK STEAK IN A LARGE RESEALABLE BAG;
SET ASIDE. IN A SMALL BOWL, WHISK TOGETHER OIL,
VINEGAR, SOY SAUCE, GARLIC AND PEPPER. POUR OVER
FLANK STEAK AND SEAL BAG. MASSAGE MARINADE OVER
STEAK AND REFRIGERATE FOR AT LEAST 4 HOURS OR
UP TO OVERNIGHT.

PREHEAT GRILL TO MEDIUM-HIGH HEAT. REMOVE
FLANK STEAK FROM MARINADE AND GRILL, TURNING
ONCE FOR ABOUT 12 MINUTES OR UNTIL MEDIUM-RARE
OR DESIRED DONENESS. REMOVE TO A CUTTING BOARD
AND TENT WITH FOIL FOR 3 MINUTES BEFORE SLICING.
SPRINKLE WITH SALT TO TASTE. TOP EACH SERVING
WITH BRUSCHETTA TO SERVE. SERVES 6.

GRILL PAN VARIATION: HEAT GRILL PAN OVER MEDIUM-HIGH HEAT AND SPRAY WITH COOKING SPRAY. GRILL AS ABOVE.

BROILER VARIATION: LINE BAKING SHEET WITH FOIL AND SET RACK IN OVEN ABOUT 6 INCHES (15 CM) FROM BROILER. PLACE STEAK ON BAKING SHEET AND BROIL ABOUT 5 MINUTES PER SIDE OR UNTIL DESIRED DONENESS.

HE WHO GOES TO BED WITHOUT EATING
WILL REGRET IT THROUGHOUT THE NIGHT.
—ITALIAN PROVERB

ITALIAN SAUSAGE AND BEEF BURGERS

WE'VE ADDED A TWIST TO THE FAVORITE JUICY GRILLED BURGER BY COMBINING HALF SAUSAGE AND HALF BEEF. HOT OR MILD ITALIAN SAUSAGES WOULD WORK EQUALLY WELL IN THIS RECIPE.

12 OZ	FRESH ITALIAN SAUSAGE MEAT	375 G
12 OZ	LEAN GROUND BEEF OR VEAL	375 G
1/2 CUP	ITALIAN SEASONED BREAD CRUMBS	125 ML
1/4 CUP	GRATED PARMESAN CHEESE	60 ML
2 TSP	WORCESTERSHIRE SAUCE	10 ML

PREHEAT BARBECUE GRILL TO MEDIUM. IN A LARGE BOWL, ADD SAUSAGE MEAT, BEEF, BREAD CRUMBS, CHEESE AND WORCESTERSHIRE SAUCE; MIX WITH YOUR HANDS UNTIL WELL COMBINED. SHAPE INTO SIX 1/2-INCH (1 CM) THICK PATTIES.

PLACE PATTIES ON GREASED GRILL AND GRILL FOR ABOUT 5 MINUTES PER SIDE OR UNTIL NO LONGER PINK INSIDE AND A MEAT THERMOMETER INSERTED HORIZONTALLY INTO THE CENTER OF A PATTY REGISTERS 160°F (71°C). SERVES 6.

TIP: SERVE WITH BUNS AND YOUR FAVORITE BURGER TOPPINGS.

HOISIN BEEF AND CABBAGE

WE ALL LOVE A STIR-FRY, BUT SOMETIMES GIVE IT A PASS BECAUSE OF THE TIME REQUIRED TO CHOP ALL THE VEGETABLES. PREPARED COLESLAW MIX CAN BE A TIME-SAVER TO HELP YOU GET A QUICK DELICIOUS MEAL ON THE TABLE.

2 TBSP	CANOLA OIL, DIVIDED	30 ML
I LB	BONELESS BEEF STEAK (SUCH AS SIRLOIN TIP OR TOP SIRLOIN) CUT INTO THIN STRIPS	500 G
5 CUPS	COLESLAW MIX	I.25 L
3 TBSP	HOISIN SAUCE	45 ML
I TBSP	CHILI GARLIC SAUCE	I5 ML
2 TSP	SESAME OIL	IO ML

IN A LARGE NONSTICK SKILLET, HEAT I TBSP (I5 ML) OIL OVER MEDIUM-HIGH HEAT. ADD HALF OF THE BEEF IN A SINGLE LAYER AND FRY FOR 2 MINUTES WITHOUT STIRRING, THEN STIR BEEF AND COOK FOR I MINUTE. TRANSFER BEEF TO A BOWL AND REPEAT WITH THE REMAINING BEEF.

IN SAME SKILLET, WITHOUT CLEANING IT, HEAT REMAINING I TBSP (I5 ML) OIL OVER MEDIUM-HIGH HEAT. ADD COLESLAW, HOISIN, CHILI GARLIC SAUCE AND SESAME OIL; STIR. COVER AND COOK FOR 3 MINUTES. UNCOVER AND ADD BEEF AND ANY ACCUMULATED JUICES TO THE SKILLET. COOK AND STIR FOR I MINUTE, OR UNTIL HEATED THROUGH. SERVES 4.

TIP: SERVE WITH HOT COOKED RICE OR NOODLES.

BEEF AND BLACK BEAN STIR-FRY

SLICE THE MEAT AGAINST THE GRAIN FOR
TENDERNESS, THEN PAT DRY FOR BETTER
BROWNING AS IT COOKS. SERVE WITH RICE
OR NOODLES TO SOP UP THE STIR-FRY JUICES.

2 TBSP	CANOLA OIL, DIVIDED	30 ML
I LB	BONELESS BEEF STEAK (SUCH AS SIRLOIN TIP OR TOP SIRLOIN) CUT INTO THIN STRIPS	500 G
5 CUPS	FROZEN STIR-FRY VEGETABLE BLEND	1.25 L
1/4 CUP	BLACK BEAN GARLIC SAUCE	60 ML
2 TSP	SESAME OIL	10 ML
2	GREEN ONIONS, SLICED	2

IN A LARGE NONSTICK SKILLET, HEAT I TBSP (15 ML) OIL
OVER MEDIUM-HIGH HEAT. ADD HALF OF THE BEEF IN
A SINGLE LAYER AND COOK FOR 3 MINUTES WITHOUT
STIRRING, THEN STIR BEEF AND COOK FOR 30 SECONDS.
TRANSFER BEEF TO A BOWL AND REPEAT WITH
THE REMAINING BEEF.

IN SAME SKILLET, WITHOUT CLEANING IT, HEAT
REMAINING I TBSP (15 ML) OIL OVER MEDIUM-HIGH HEAT.
SAUTÈ FROZEN VEGETABLES FOR 6 MINUTES, SCRAPING
UP ANY BROWNED FLAVOR BITS IN THE PAN. COVER AND
COOK I MINUTE. UNCOVER AND ADD BLACK BEAN SAUCE,
SESAME OIL, GREEN ONIONS, BEEF AND ANY ACCUMULATED
MEAT JUICES. COOK AND STIR FOR I MINUTE, OR UNTIL
HEATED THROUGH. SERVES 4.

TIP: FROZEN STIR-FRY VEGETABLE MIX IS SO CONVENIENT
TO USE. BLENDS ARE LABELED IN A VARIETY OF WAYS,
SUCH AS ASIAN VEGETABLES AND ASIAN BLEND.

MIDDLE EASTERN MEATLOAF

MEATLOAF GETS A FLAVOR MAKEOVER WHEN ZA'ATAR IS ADDED TO THE MIX. ZA'ATAR IS A BLEND OF DRIED HERBS SUCH AS THYME, OREGANO AND MARJORAM, ALONG WITH SESAME SEEDS, CUMIN AND CORIANDER. LOOK FOR THIS SPICE BLEND IN THE INTERNATIONAL AISLE OF THE GROCERY STORE. PRECOOKING THE ONION GIVES THE MEATLOAF A MORE TENDER TEXTURE AND AN ADDED BOOST OF FLAVOR.

2 TSP	CANOLA OIL	10 ML
1	ONION, GRATED	1
2	LARGE EGGS, BEATEN	2
1 CUP	DRIED BREAD CRUMBS	250 ML
3/4 CUP	ZA'ATAR SPICE MIX	175 ML
2 LBS	LEAN GROUND BEEF OR VEAL	1 KG

PREHEAT OVEN TO 375°F (190°C). IN A NONSTICK SKILLET, HEAT OIL OVER MEDIUM HEAT. FRY ONION FOR ABOUT 8 MINUTES, UNTIL SOFTENED AND BEGINNING TO BROWN. SCRAPE INTO A LARGE BOWL AND LET COOL SLIGHTLY. STIR IN EGGS, BREAD CRUMBS AND ZA'ATAR UNTIL COMBINED. ADD BEEF; USING HANDS, MIX UNTIL WELL COMBINED. PRESS MIXTURE INTO 9- BY 5-INCH (23 BY 12.5 CM) LOAF PAN.

BAKE FOR ABOUT 55 TO 60 MINUTES OR UNTIL A MEAT THERMOMETER INSERTED IN THE CENTER REGISTERS 165°F (74°C). LET STAND FOR 5 MINUTES BEFORE SLICING. SERVES 8.

TIP: THIS MEATLOAF IS EXTRA TASTY SANDWICHED BETWEEN SLICES OF BREAD OR IN A PITA.

ROAST BEEF SALAD ROLLS

FASTER THAN TAKEOUT, THESE FRESH HAND-HELD SALAD ROLLS ARE EASY TO MAKE. GET YOUR FAMILY AND FRIENDS TOGETHER SO EVERYONE CAN MAKE THEIR OWN. PEANUT DIPPING SAUCES CAN VARY IN VISCOSITY. IF THE BRAND YOU USE IS TOO THICK, STIR IN A LITTLE WATER TO THIN IT OUT A BIT.

12	ROUND RICE PAPER WRAPPERS (8 INCHES/20 CM)	12
2 CUPS	SHREDDED LETTUCE	500 ML
I CUP	GRATED CARROT	250 ML
12 OZ	THINLY SLICED LEFTOVER ROAST BEEF, CUT INTO STRIPS	375 G
6 TBSP	PREPARED PEANUT SATAY SAUCE OR HOISIN SAUCE	90 ML

IN A PIE PLATE OR SHALLOW DISH FILLED WITH WARM WATER, SOAK ONE RICE WRAPPER FOR ABOUT 20 SECONDS, OR UNTIL IT BECOMES PLIABLE. PLACE ON A FLAT WORK SURFACE. SOAK A SECOND RICE PAPER SHEET AND PLACE IT ON TOP OF THE FIRST SHEET. (THIS CREATES A STRONGER WRAPPER THAT IS STURDIER FOR ROLLING.)

ARRANGE SOME LETTUCE, CARROT AND ROAST BEEF ON THE BOTTOM HALF OF THE WRAPPER. DRIZZLE WITH I TBSP (15 ML) SAUCE. CAREFULLY AND FIRMLY ROLL UP THE PAPER TO ENCLOSE FILLING AND CREATE A CYLINDER, TUCKING IN THE SIDES AS YOU ROLL (LIKE ROLLING A BURRITO). TRY NOT TO OVERFILL, AS THIS MAKES IT DIFFICULT TO ROLL UP. REPEAT WITH REMAINING INGREDIENTS.

SERVE WITH EXTRA PEANUT SAUCE FOR DIPPING. ROLLS ARE BEST EATEN IMMEDIATELY, BUT YOU CAN COVER THE WRAPPERS WITH PLASTIC WRAP AND REFRIGERATE FOR UP TO 2 HOURS. MAKES 6 ROLLS.

TIP: FOLLOW YOUR TASTE BUDS AND ADD IN OTHER FAVORITE FLAVORS, SUCH AS SRIRACHA, CILANTRO, GREEN ONION, CUCUMBER, SWEET BELL PEPPERS OR PEANUTS.

TIP: FIND RICE PAPER WRAPPERS IN THE INTERNATIONAL SECTION OF THE GROCERY STORE.

I FINALLY GOT RID OF WINTER FAT
— NOW I HAVE SPRING ROLLS.

BEEF AND LENTIL BURGERS

WE GIVE THIS BURGER A THUMBS-UP FOR FLAVOR AND TEXTURE. WE'VE USED CANNED LENTILS FOR THIS RECIPE, BUT IF YOU HAVE A PANTRY FULL OF DRIED LENTILS, GO AHEAD AND COOK UP A BATCH.

1	CAN (19 OZ/540 ML) COOKED LENTILS, DRAINED (2 CUPS/500 ML)	1
1 LB	LEAN GROUND BEEF OR VEAL	500 G
1/4 CUP	SEASONED ITALIAN BREAD CRUMBS	60 ML
1 1/2 TSP	ONION POWDER	7 ML
1	LARGE EGG, BEATEN	1
1/2 TSP	EACH SALT AND BLACK PEPPER	2 ML

PREHEAT BARBECUE GRILL TO MEDIUM-HIGH. IN A LARGE BOWL, ADD LENTILS, BEEF, BREAD CRUMBS, ONION POWDER, EGG, SALT AND PEPPER; MIX WITH YOUR HANDS UNTIL WELL COMBINED. SHAPE INTO SIX 3/4-INCH (2 CM) THICK PATTIES. IF A FEW LENTILS FALL OUT, JUST PRESS THEM BACK INTO PATTY. PLACE ON A BAKING TRAY AND REFRIGERATE 10 MINUTES.

PLACE PATTIES ON GREASED GRILL AND GRILL FOR ABOUT 4 MINUTES PER SIDE OR UNTIL NO LONGER PINK INSIDE AND A MEAT THERMOMETER INSERTED HORIZONTALLY INTO THE CENTER OF A PATTY REGISTERS 160°C (71°C). SERVES 6.

TIP: SERVE WITH LETTUCE OR ON GREENS FOR A BUNLESS BURGER OPTION.

SKILLET BEEF FAST-FRY STEAKS WITH TOMATOES AND OLIVES

THIS IS A QUICK, FLAVORFUL WAY TO PREPARE BEEF DURING THE WEEK. IF YOU HAVE SOME LEFTOVER COOKED VEGETABLES, ADD THEM TO THE SAUCE TO USE UP WHAT'S IN THE FRIDGE.

1 TBSP	CANOLA OIL	15 ML
8 OZ	BEEF FAST-FRY STRIPLOIN STEAK OR MINUTE STEAKS	250 G
1/2 TSP	EACH SALT AND BLACK PEPPER, DIVIDED	2 ML
1	ONION, CHOPPED	1
2	GARLIC CLOVES, MINCED	2
2 CUPS	GRAPE TOMATOES, SLICED IN HALF	500 ML
1/2 CUP	PITTED HALVED GREEN OLIVES	125 ML

IN A SKILLET, HEAT OIL OVER MEDIUM-HIGH HEAT AND COOK CUTLETS FOR ABOUT 5 MINUTES, TURNING ONCE OR UNTIL BROWNED. REMOVE TO PLATE AND SPRINKLE WITH HALF OF THE SALT AND PEPPER.

RETURN SKILLET TO MEDIUM HEAT AND COOK ONION AND GARLIC FOR 5 MINUTES OR UNTIL SOFTENED. ADD TOMATOES AND REMAINING SALT AND PEPPER; COOK FOR 5 MINUTES. STIR IN OLIVES AND COOK FOR 1 MINUTE. RETURN BEEF TO SAUCE AND STIR TO COAT WITH SAUCE. MAKES 2 SERVINGS.

VARIATIONS: YOU CAN SUBSTITUTE VEAL OR PORK CUTLETS FOR THE BEEF.

HARISSA BEEF SKEWERS

LOOK FOR HARISSA IN THE SPICE AISLE AS A PASTE IN A TUBE OR JAR AND ALSO AS A DRY SPICE MIX. IT PACKS SOME HEAT BUT IS FULL OF SPICE FLAVOR THAT COULD INCLUDE CUMIN AND CORIANDER. A WONDERFUL AROMA WILL BE WAFTING INTO THE NEIGHBORS' YARD AS YOU GRILL, SO MAKE ROOM AT THE TABLE FOR SUDDEN GUESTS.

2 TBSP	CANOLA OIL	30 ML
2 TBSP	HARISSA PASTE (OR 1/2 TSP/2 ML HARISSA SPICE)	30 ML
1/2 TSP	SALT	2 ML
1/4 TSP	BLACK PEPPER	1 ML
1 1/2 LBS	BEEF TOP SIRLOIN STEAK, CUT INTO 1 1/2 INCH (3.5 CM) CUBES	750 G
1 CUP	RED PEPPER HUMMUS	250 ML
6	WHOLE WHEAT PITAS	6
1 1/2 CUPS	SHREDDED ROMAINE LETTUCE	375 ML

IN A LARGE BOWL, WHISK TOGETHER OIL, HARISSA, SALT AND PEPPER. STIR IN BEEF TO COAT. COVER AND REFRIGERATE FOR AT LEAST 30 MINUTES OR OVERNIGHT. MEANWHILE, IF USING BAMBOO SKEWERS, SOAK IN WATER FOR 30 MINUTES.

PREHEAT GRILL TO MEDIUM-HIGH. THREAD BEEF ONTO SKEWERS; DISCARD ANY MARINADE. GRILL SKEWERS, TURNING ONCE, FOR ABOUT 6 MINUTES FOR MEDIUM RARE OR TO DESIRED DONENESS.

SPREAD HUMMUS ON PITAS AND TOP EACH WITH BEEF SKEWER AND LETTUCE. SERVES 6.

TIP: THERE'S A GREAT VARIETY OF HUMMUS AVAILABLE IN THE GROCERY STORES; CHOOSE YOUR FAVORITE FLAVOR OR USE HOMEMADE HUMMUS INSTEAD.

IT'S GETTIN' HOT IN HERE,
SO TAKE OFF ALL YOUR CLOVES.

SPICY SHREDDED BEEF TACOS

HAVE THE SHREDDED BEEF READY FOR WHEN YOU GET HOME FROM WORK TO FILL HARD OR SOFT SHELL TACOS FOR A KIDS' FAVORITE. WITH A FEW INGREDIENTS ADDED, THE BEEF HAS GREAT FLAVOR. IT CAN BE MADE AHEAD AND ENJOYED FOR ANOTHER NIGHT'S DINNER OR USED AS A TOPPING FOR SALAD OR EVEN AS AN APPETIZER TO SHARE WITH GUESTS.

2 TBSP	CANOLA OIL	30 ML
2 TBSP	PERI PERI SPICE MIXTURE OR CAJUN SPICE MIX	30 ML
1	BONELESS SIRLOIN TIP BEEF OR VEAL ROAST (ABOUT 2 LBS/1 KG)	1
1	JAR (2¾ CUPS/700 ML) TOMATO BASIL PASTA SAUCE, OR SEE PASTA SAUCE (PAGE 207)	1
PINCH	EACH SALT AND BLACK PEPPER (OPTIONAL)	PINCH
2	PACKAGES (4½ OZ/133 G EACH) HARD TORTILLAS, OR 2 BAGS (11 OZ/340 G EACH) SMALL FLOUR TORTILLAS	2
1 CUP	SOUR CREAM	250 ML

IN A SMALL BOWL, COMBINE OIL WITH SPICE MIXTURE AND RUB HALF OF IT ALL OVER ROAST. HEAT A LARGE NONSTICK SKILLET AND BROWN ROAST ON ALL SIDES. PLACE IN SLOW COOKER. ADD PASTA SAUCE AND REMAINING SPICE MIXTURE TO SKILLET AND BRING TO THE BOIL, SCRAPING UP BROWN BITS. POUR INTO SLOW COOKER. COVER AND COOK ON LOW FOR 8 TO 10 HOURS, OR ALTERNATIVELY ON HIGH FOR 4 TO 5 HOURS, UNTIL MEAT IS VERY TENDER. (IF POSSIBLE, TURN MEAT TWO TIMES TO SUBMERGE IN THE LIQUID SO EXPOSED SIDE WILL NOT DRY OUT.)

REMOVE ROAST FROM JUICE AND LET STAND FOR 10 MINUTES. USING TWO FORKS, PULL ROAST APART AND RETURN TO SLOW COOKER; STIR INTO SAUCE TO COMBINE. SEASON WITH SALT AND PEPPER, IF NEEDED.

FILL TACO SHELLS WITH BEEF MIXTURE AND TOP WITH SOUR CREAM AND OTHER TOPPINGS AS DESIRED.

MAKES 18 TACOS OR ABOUT 8 SERVINGS.

TIP: CHOPPED TOMATOES AND CHOPPED AVOCADO MAKE GOOD ADDITIONS OR SUBSTITUTIONS FOR THE SOUR CREAM.

DO YOU WANT TO TACO 'BOUT IT?
IT'S NACHO PROBLEM.

SMOKED BEEF BRISKET

THIS DELICIOUS, SLOW-COOKED BEEF FAVORITE
IS WORTH THE WAIT FOR MELT-IN-YOUR-MOUTH
TENDER BRISKET. MAKE THIS FOR A LARGE SUMMER
GATHERING OR FAMILY GET-TOGETHER. LEFTOVERS
ARE ALWAYS WELCOME FOR SMOKED BRISKET
SANDWICHES PILED HIGH THE NEXT DAY!

1	BEEF BRISKET (ABOUT 6 TO 8 LBS/ 3 TO 4 KG)	1
1/2 CUP	MONTREAL STEAK SPICE	125 ML
1 TBSP	GARLIC POWDER	15 ML
1 TBSP	ONION POWDER	15 ML
1	CAN (14 OZ/440 ML) STOUT BEER	1

TRIM SOME OF THE HARD FAT OFF THE BRISKET. USING A
MEAT MALLET OR YOUR FISTS, POUND BRISKET TO EVEN
IT OUT TO A SIMILAR THICKNESS ALL OVER.

IN A SMALL BOWL, COMBINE STEAK SPICE, GARLIC
AND ONION POWDER. IN A LARGE BAKING SHEET OR
DISPOSABLE ALUMINUM PAN, SEASON ALL SIDES OF THE
BRISKET GENEROUSLY WITH SPICE MIXTURE. COVER WITH
PLASTIC WRAP AND REFRIGERATE FOR 12 TO 24 HOURS.

PREPARE YOUR CHARCOAL SMOKER TO 225°F (107°C)
AND PLACE AN ALUMINUM TRAY WITH WATER UNDER
THE GRILL GRATE TO KEEP THE DIRECT HEAT DOWN; IT
WILL ALSO CATCH THE WONDERFUL JUICES THAT DRIP
FROM THE BRISKET. FILL A SPRAY OR MISTER BOTTLE
WITH THE BEER. IF USING AN ELECTRIC PELLET SMOKER,
SET IT TO 225°F (107°C).

PLACE BRISKET FAT SIDE UP, DIRECTLY ON THE GRILL, OVER A FOIL TRAY IF USING CHARCOAL SMOKER. SPRAY BRISKET EVERY HOUR, THROUGH THE FIRST 4 OR 5 HOURS. THIS WILL KEEP THE OUTSIDE OF THE BRISKET COOLER DURING THE SMOKING PHASE, SO YOU GET GOOD SMOKE PENETRATION.

USING A MEAT THERMOMETER INSERTED AT THE THICKEST PART OF THE BRISKET, CHECK TEMPERATURE AND, ONCE BRISKET REACHES ABOUT 165°F (74°C), REMOVE IT FROM GRILL AND WRAP IT WITH BUTCHER'S PAPER OR FOIL. PLACE WRAPPED BRISKET IN LARGE ALUMINUM PAN TO CATCH ALL THE JUICES. CONTINUE TO COOK, MAKING SURE TEMPERATURE IS STILL 225°F (107°C), FOR APPROXIMATELY 4 HOURS OR UNTIL IT REACHES INTERNAL TEMPERATURE OF 203°F (95°C). REMOVE FROM HEAT AND PLACE IN A COOLER OR COLD OVEN TO REST FOR A COUPLE OF HOURS. UNWRAP AND SLICE TO SERVE. SERVES 12 TO 16.

TIP: BRISKETS CAN TAKE ANYWHERE BETWEEN 10 TO 18 HOURS TO COOK PLUS A FEW HOURS TO REST. YOU WILL WANT TO WORK BACKWARD FROM WHEN YOU WOULD LIKE TO SERVE IT. IT IS IMPORTANT TO HAVE THE BRISKET REST, SO IF IT LOOKS AS IF IT IS GOING TO FINISH TOO SOON, DIAL BACK THE TEMPERATURE ON YOUR GRILL TO 200°F (93°C) TO SLOW DOWN THE COOK.

CONTINUED ON NEXT PAGE

TIP: WHEN USING A CHARCOAL SMOKER, ENSURE THAT THERE IS ENOUGH FUEL (WOOD CHUNKS AND CHARCOAL) TO LAST FOR THE ENTIRE COOK. IT'S BETTER TO HAVE MORE FUEL THAN NECESSARY THAN IT IS TO HAVE TO DISMANTLE YOUR GRILL TO ADD MORE FUEL DURING THE COOK. IF YOU ARE USING AN ELECTRIC SMOKER, YOU WILL BE ABLE TO ADD MORE PELLETS EASILY DURING THE COOK.

TIP: WHEN THE BRISKET REACHES 165°F (74°C), THIS IS REFERRED TO AS "THE STALL." THE FAT STARTS TO RENDER AT THIS TEMPERATURE. WRAPPING IT WILL HELP GET THE BRISKET THROUGH THIS TEMPERATURE BARRIER.

CHICKEN AND TURKEY

JERK CHICKEN WRAPS

THIS RECIPE IS A FAVORITE WITH SYLVIA'S FAMILY. A LITTLE HEAT AND A HINT OF SWEET DESCRIBE THIS TASTY SANDWICH. FEEL FREE TO EXPERIMENT AND ADD EXTRAS LIKE AVOCADO, SHREDDED LETTUCE, CILANTRO OR COLESLAW.

8	SKIN-ON, BONE-IN CHICKEN THIGHS	8
1½ to 2 TBSP	CARIBBEAN JERK SPICE PASTE	22 to 30 ML
1 TBSP	CANOLA OIL	15 ML
½ TSP	SALT	2 ML
1	RED ONION, THINLY SLICED	1
⅓ CUP	MANGO CHUTNEY	75 ML
8	GARLIC NAAN	8

IN A 13- BY 9-INCH (33 BY 23 CM) CASSEROLE DISH, PLACE CHICKEN, JERK SPICE PASTE, OIL, SALT AND ONION. USING YOUR HANDS, THOROUGHLY MIX THE INGREDIENTS TOGETHER SO CHICKEN IS FULLY COATED. COVER AND REFRIGERATE AT LEAST 3 HOURS OR OVERNIGHT.

REMOVE CHICKEN FROM REFRIGERATOR AND PREHEAT OVEN TO 400°F (200°C). ARRANGE CHICKEN, SKIN SIDE UP, IN A SINGLE LAYER AND BAKE FOR ABOUT 40 MINUTES, OR UNTIL A MEAT THERMOMETER INSERTED IN THE THICKEST PART OF CHICKEN REGISTERS 165°F (74°C). LET CHICKEN COOL SLIGHTLY, THEN REMOVE MEAT FROM THE BONES AND SHRED INTO LARGE PIECES. DISCARD BONES AND MIX THE CHICKEN WITH ANY JUICES FROM THE DISH. DIVIDE THE CHICKEN, ONIONS AND THE CHUTNEY ONTO THE NAAN. ROLL UP TO SERVE. SERVES 8.

TIP: NAAN IS AN INDIAN FLAT BREAD. AN OPTION IS TO SERVE THE WRAPS IN WARM NAAN. HEAT EACH NAAN FOR 30 SECONDS IN THE MICROWAVE OR WRAP NAAN IN FOIL AND PLACE IN AN OVEN, PREHEATED TO 400°F (200 °C) FOR 4 TO 5 MINUTES, OR JUST UNTIL WARM.

TIP: THE MARINATING CHICKEN CAN BE FROZEN. THAW OVERNIGHT IN THE FRIDGE AND BAKE AS DIRECTED.

TIP: THIS SHREDDED CHICKEN ALSO TASTES GREAT SERVED OVER HOT COOKED RICE OR QUINOA.

DINNER CHOICES: 1. TAKE IT. 2. LEAVE IT.

SWEET AND SPICY
GRILLED CHICKEN SKEWERS

MARINATING THE CHICKEN ENSURES THAT IT IS
FULL OF FLAVOR. THE SAUCE CARAMELIZES AND
SLIGHTLY CHARS TO CREATE A SWEET, SMOKY LAYER
ON THE CHICKEN. STEAMED RICE AND GREEN BEANS
WOULD PAIR PERFECTLY WITH THIS DISH.

8	BONELESS, SKINLESS CHICKEN THIGHS, CUT INTO 1½-INCH (4 CM) PIECES	8
½ CUP	SWEET THAI CHILI SAUCE, DIVIDED	125 ML
2 TBSP	SOY SAUCE	30 ML
2 TBSP	CANOLA OIL	30 ML
2 TBSP	SRIRACHA	30 ML
I TBSP	GRATED FRESH GINGER	15 ML

IN A LARGE BOWL, COMBINE CHICKEN, ¼ CUP (60 ML) CHILI
SAUCE, SOY SAUCE, OIL, SRIRACHA AND GINGER. COVER AND
REFRIGERATE I HOUR.

PREHEAT GREASED BARBECUE GRILL TO MEDIUM.
REMOVE CHICKEN FROM REFRIGERATOR AND THREAD ONTO
METAL SKEWERS, DISCARDING MARINADE. GRILL SKEWERS
FOR 8 TO IO MINUTES, TURNING EVERY FEW MINUTES,
UNTIL CHICKEN IS NO LONGER PINK INSIDE. BRUSH
CHICKEN WITH REMAINING ¼ CUP (60 ML) CHILI SAUCE
JUST BEFORE SERVING. SERVES 4.

TIP: SWEET THAI CHILI SAUCE IS SOMETIMES SOLD AS
DIPPING SAUCE FOR SPRING ROLLS AND EGG ROLLS.

Southwestern Beef Meatball Soup (page 65)

Lemongrass Shrimp Soup (page 68)

Chunky Chicken Minestrone (page 69)

Beef and Black Bean Stir-Fry (page 80)

Roast Beef Salad Rolls (page 82)

Skillet Beef Fast-Fry Steaks with Tomatoes and Olives (page 85)

Grilled Peanut Butter Pineapple Chicken Skewers (page 104)

Jerk Chicken and Sweet Potato Sheet-Pan Supper (page 108)

SALSA CHICKEN

WHEN YOU HAVE STAPLES ON HAND, MAKING DINNER CAN BE EASY. SALSA IS A WONDERFUL WAY TO ADD FLAVOR TO MOST MEALS, WHETHER YOU COOK WITH IT OR SERVE IT ALONGSIDE.

2 TBSP	CANOLA OIL, DIVIDED	30 ML
2 TSP	CHILI POWDER	10 ML
1/4 TSP	EACH SALT AND BLACK PEPPER	1 ML
4	BONELESS SKINLESS CHICKEN BREASTS (ABOUT 1 1/2 LB/750 G)	4
1 CUP	SALSA	250 ML
3/4 CUP	SHREDDED CHEDDAR MOZZARELLA BLEND	175 ML
1/2 CUP	COARSELY CRUSHED FLAVORED TORTILLA CHIPS	125 ML

PREHEAT OVEN TO 400°F (200°C). IN A LARGE BOWL, STIR TOGETHER 1 TBSP (15 ML) OIL, CHILI POWDER, SALT AND PEPPER. ADD CHICKEN AND TURN TO COAT EVENLY.

IN A LARGE OVENPROOF SKILLET, HEAT REMAINING OIL OVER MEDIUM-HIGH HEAT. BROWN CHICKEN ON BOTH SIDES AND REMOVE SKILLET FROM HEAT. POUR SALSA ALL OVER CHICKEN AND SPRINKLE WITH CHEESE AND CHIPS.

PLACE SKILLET IN OVEN FOR ABOUT 15 MINUTES OR UNTIL CHICKEN IS NO LONGER PINK AND CHEESE IS BUBBLY AND GOLDEN. SERVES 4.

TIP: FOR A SPICIER VERSION, USE HOT SALSA AND SPICY TORTILLA CHIPS. FOR ADDED ZIP, USE A TEX-MEX BLEND OF SHREDDED CHEESE.

JAPANESE CHICKEN CUTLETS

THIS POPULAR DISH IS ALSO KNOWN AS CHICKEN KATSU. SERVE CRISPY CHICKEN WITH HOT COOKED RICE, SHREDDED CABBAGE AND A WEDGE OF LEMON.

I LB	BONELESS SKINLESS CHICKEN BREASTS	500 G
1/2 TSP	EACH SALT AND BLACK PEPPER	2 ML
1/2 CUP	ALL-PURPOSE FLOUR	125 ML
2	LARGE EGGS, BEATEN	2
1 1/2 CUPS	PANKO BREAD CRUMBS	375 ML
1/2 CUP	CANOLA OIL	125 ML
	TONKATSU SAUCE	

CUT CHICKEN BREASTS HORIZONTALLY INTO THIN CUTLETS, THEN SEASON WITH SALT AND PEPPER ON BOTH SIDES. PLACE FLOUR IN A SHALLOW DISH, EGGS IN ANOTHER AND PANKO IN A THIRD. DREDGE EACH CUTLET IN FLOUR, DIP IN EGGS, THEN PRESS IN PANKO TO COAT. PLACE ON A PLATE. DISCARD ANY EXCESS FLOUR, EGGS AND PANKO.

IN A SKILLET, HEAT 1/4 CUP (60 ML) OIL OVER MEDIUM HEAT. ADD TWO CUTLETS AND COOK, TURNING ONCE, FOR 2 TO 3 MINUTES PER SIDE OR UNTIL COATING IS GOLDEN AND CRISPY AND CHICKEN IS COOKED THROUGH. TRANSFER CUTLETS TO A BAKING SHEET LINED WITH PAPER TOWELS AND KEEP WARM IN A 200°F (100°C) OVEN. REPEAT WITH THE REMAINING OIL AND CUTLETS.

SEASON WITH ADDITIONAL SALT, IF DESIRED. CUT CHICKEN INTO THIN STRIPS AND SERVE WITH TONKATSU SAUCE. SERVES 4.

TIP: PANKO ARE LIGHT AND CRISP JAPANESE BREAD CRUMBS. YOU CAN USE REGULAR OR WHOLE WHEAT PANKO IN THIS RECIPE.

TIP: TONKATSU SAUCE IS A THICK JAPANESE WORCESTERSHIRE SAUCE. IT IS AVAILABLE IN BOTTLES IN THE ASIAN FOOD AISLE OF MANY GROCERY STORES.

TIP: LEFTOVERS CAN BE STORED IN THE FRIDGE FOR UP TO 4 DAYS. TO REWARM, PLACE IN A PREHEATED 400°F (200°C) OVEN FOR 10 TO 12 MINUTES OR UNTIL HEATED THROUGH.

TIP: YOU CAN ALSO ENJOY THIS CRISPY CHICKEN IN A SANDWICH.

I'M SOY INTO YOU.

EVERYTHING BAGEL
SPICE CHICKEN DINNER

THIS COZY MEAL OF CHICKEN BAKED IN THE
OVEN ALONG WITH VEGGIES AND SIDES IS
PERFECT FOR A BUSY WEEKNIGHT OR A RELAXING
WEEKEND. TO MAKE CLEANUP EASIER, LINE
THE BAKING SHEET WITH PARCHMENT PAPER.

2 LBS	BONE-IN SKIN-ON CHICKEN THIGHS	1 KG
4 CUPS	BROCCOLI FLORETS, CUT INTO BITE-SIZE PIECES	1 L
1 LB	MINI POTATOES, SLICED IN HALF	500 G
1	CAN (19 OZ/540 ML) CHICKPEAS, RINSED AND DRAINED WELL (2 CUPS/500 ML)	1
2 TBSP	CANOLA OIL	30 ML
1/2 TSP	EACH SALT AND BLACK PEPPER	2 ML
1 1/2 TO 2 TBSP	EVERYTHING BAGEL SPICE MIX	22 TO 30 ML

PREHEAT OVEN TO 450°F (230°C). ON A LARGE RIMMED
BAKING SHEET, PLACE CHICKEN, BROCCOLI, POTATOES
AND CHICKPEAS. DRIZZLE WITH OIL AND TOSS TO COAT.
SPRINKLE WITH SALT AND PEPPER.

SPREAD IN A SINGLE LAYER AND ARRANGE CHICKEN
PIECES SKIN SIDE UP. BAKE FOR 30 TO 40 MINUTES, OR
UNTIL CHICKEN IS COOKED THROUGH AND VEGETABLES
ARE TENDER. REMOVE FROM OVEN, TOSS TO COAT IN
COOKING JUICES, THEN EVENLY SPRINKLE THE SPICE
MIX ON TOP. SERVES 6.

TIP: LARGE POTATOES CUT INTO SMALL, BITE-SIZE PIECES CAN BE SUBSTITUTED FOR MINI POTATOES.

TIP: IF YOU DO NOT HAVE A LARGE BAKING SHEET, USE TWO SMALLER BAKING SHEETS, ROTATING THEM HALFWAY THROUGH BAKING TIME.

YOU NEED TO BE AS GOOD AS BREAD AND WINE.

TAHINI HONEY CHICKEN

TAHINI IS THE TOASTED SESAME SEED PASTE
THAT GIVES THIS CHICKEN A WONDERFUL NUTTY
FLAVOR. SERVE WITH A SALAD ON THE SIDE.

1/4 CUP	TAHINI	60 ML
1/4 CUP	HONEY GARLIC SAUCE	60 ML
1	LEMON, ZESTED AND JUICED	1
8	BONELESS, SKINLESS CHICKEN THIGHS, PATTED DRY	8
1/2 TSP	EACH SALT AND BLACK PEPPER	2 ML
2	GREEN ONIONS, CHOPPED	2

LINE A BAKING SHEET WITH PARCHMENT PAPER. IN A
MEDIUM BOWL, COMBINE TAHINI, HONEY GARLIC SAUCE,
LEMON ZEST, LEMON JUICE, CHICKEN, SALT, PEPPER AND
GREEN ONIONS. MARINATE IN THE REFRIGERATOR FOR
1 HOUR.

PREHEAT OVEN TO 400°F (200°C). PLACE CHICKEN
ON PREPARED BAKING SHEET AND BAKE FOR 30 TO
35 MINUTES, OR UNTIL CHICKEN IS COOKED THROUGH
AND REGISTERS 165°F (74°C). SERVE WITH LEMON WEDGES
ON THE SIDE. SERVES 4.

TIP: ANY CHICKEN LEFTOVERS MAKE A TASTY
SANDWICH FILLING.

PAUL'S FAVORITE
SOY SAUCE CHICKEN

THIS IS ONE OF SYLVIA'S HUSBAND'S FAVORITE DISHES FROM HIS CHILDHOOD. WE'VE ALL BEEN TAUGHT TO NOT OPEN THE LID DURING SLOW-COOKING; HOWEVER, IN THIS CASE, THE CHICKEN IS COOKED THROUGH AFTER 2 HOURS AND THE LAST 30 MINUTES ALLOWS THE FLAVORS TO DEEPEN.

I CUP	SOY SAUCE	250 ML
1/2 CUP	GRANULATED SUGAR	125 ML
1/4 CUP	WATER	60 ML
I TBSP	FIVE-SPICE POWDER	15 ML
8	GARLIC CLOVES, SLICED IN HALF	8
3 LBS	BONE-IN SKIN-ON CHICKEN THIGHS OR DRUMSTICKS	1.5 KG

IN A 6-QUART SLOW COOKER, STIR TOGETHER THE SOY SAUCE, SUGAR, WATER, FIVE-SPICE POWDER AND GARLIC. ADD CHICKEN AND STIR TO COAT. ARRANGE THE CHICKEN PIECES SKIN SIDE DOWN. COVER AND COOK ON HIGH FOR 2 HOURS. GIVE THE CHICKEN A STIR, TURNING THE PIECES OVER, AND COOK ANOTHER 30 MINUTES. SERVES 6 TO 8.

TIP: STORE ANY LEFTOVER CHICKEN SEPARATELY FROM THE COOKING LIQUID, AS THE CHICKEN WILL CONTINUE TO ABSORB THE SAUCE AND MAY BECOME TOO SALTY.

TIP: THE RECIPE CREATES PLENTY OF SAUCE, MAKING IT PERFECT FOR SERVING OVER STEAMED RICE AND VEGETABLES. THE SAUCE KEEPS FOR 5 DAYS IN THE REFRIGERATOR AND CAN ALSO BE USED FOR ADDING TO STIR-FRIES OR FRIED RICE.

GRILLED PEANUT BUTTER PINEAPPLE CHICKEN SKEWERS

HAVE SOME FUN AND CHANGE UP YOUR CHICKEN DINNER WITH THIS COMBINATION OF SWEET AND SALTY. PEANUT BUTTER MAKES A GREAT FLAVOR ADDITION TO THIS MARINADE.

1/3 CUP	PEANUT BUTTER	75 ML
1/4 CUP	WARM WATER	60 ML
1/2 CUP	SWEET THAI CHILI SAUCE, DIVIDED	125 ML
2 TBSP	CHOPPED FRESH CILANTRO	30 ML
1/4 TSP	EACH SALT AND BLACK PEPPER	1 ML
1 LB	BONELESS SKINLESS CHICKEN BREASTS (ABOUT 2)	500 G
HALF	FRESH CORED PINEAPPLE	HALF

IN A LARGE BOWL, WHISK TOGETHER PEANUT BUTTER, WATER, 1/4 CUP (60 ML) OF THE THAI CHILI SAUCE, CILANTRO, SALT AND PEPPER. CUT CHICKEN INTO 1-INCH (2.5 CM) CUBES AND ADD TO BOWL, TOSSING WELL TO COAT. COVER AND REFRIGERATE FOR AT LEAST 1 HOUR OR OVERNIGHT.

PREHEAT GRILL TO MEDIUM HEAT. MEANWHILE, IF USING BAMBOO SKEWERS, SOAK THEM IN WATER FOR 30 MINUTES.

CUT PINEAPPLE INTO 1-INCH (2.5 CM) CUBES. SKEWER CHICKEN AND PINEAPPLE ONTO SKEWERS. GRILL, TURNING OCCASIONALLY, FOR 12 TO 15 MINUTES OR UNTIL CHICKEN IS NO LONGER PINK INSIDE. SERVE WITH REMAINING THAI CHILI SAUCE. SERVES 4.

GRILLED MARINATED CHICKEN BREASTS

THIS LARGE BATCH OF CHICKEN IS PERFECT TO GET YOU READY FOR THE WEEK. ENJOY THEM AS THEY ARE OR IN OTHER RECIPES.

1/4 CUP	CANOLA OIL	60 ML
3	GARLIC CLOVES, MINCED	3
1 TBSP	LEMON JUICE OR WHITE WINE VINEGAR	15 ML
1 TBSP	DRIED OREGANO	15 ML
2 TSP	CHILI POWDER	10 ML
1/2 TSP	SALT	2 ML
2 LBS	BONELESS, SKINLESS CHICKEN BREASTS	1 KG

IN A LARGE SHALLOW DISH, STIR TOGETHER OIL, GARLIC, LEMON JUICE, OREGANO, CHILI POWDER AND SALT. ADD CHICKEN AND TURN TO COAT WELL. COVER AND REFRIGERATE FOR AT LEAST 30 MINUTES OR OVERNIGHT.

PREHEAT GRILL TO MEDIUM. GRILL CHICKEN ON OILED GRILL FOR ABOUT 12 MINUTES, TURNING ONCE, UNTIL NO LONGER PINK INSIDE. ENJOY AS IS OR INCORPORATE THEM INTO YOUR FAVORITE SALAD OR SANDWICH. OR FREEZE TO USE LATER IN A SOUP OR STIR-FRY! SERVES 8.

TIP: IF YOU DON'T WANT TO GRILL ALL THE CHICKEN RIGHT AWAY, YOU CAN FREEZE HALF IN THE MARINADE FOR UP TO 2 WEEKS. YOU CAN ALSO GRILL THEM ALL AND REFRIGERATE FOR UP TO 3 DAYS, OR FREEZE THEM.

CHICKEN TAPENADE PUFF ROLLS

*THESE CAN BE ENJOYED IN LARGER SERVINGS
LIKE SAUSAGE ROLLS OR CUT INTO SMALLER
PIECES TO SERVE UP AS APPETIZERS.*

8 OZ	GROUND CHICKEN OR TURKEY	250 G
1/3 CUP	SEASONED BREAD CRUMBS	75 ML
1/3 CUP	OLIVE TAPENADE OR SUN-DRIED TOMATO PESTO	75 ML
2	GARLIC CLOVES, MINCED	2
1/4 TSP	EACH SALT AND BLACK PEPPER	1 ML
8 OZ	PUFF PASTRY	250 G

IN A BOWL, MIX TOGETHER CHICKEN WITH BREAD CRUMBS, TAPENADE, GARLIC, SALT AND PEPPER UNTIL WELL COMBINED. PREHEAT OVEN TO 400°F (200°C).

ROLL OUT PUFF PASTRY INTO A 12- BY 10-INCH (30 BY 25 CM) RECTANGLE ON A LIGHTLY FLOURED SURFACE. CUT IN HALF CROSSWISE; DIVIDE CHICKEN MIXTURE ONTO THE TWO PIECES. SHAPE EACH INTO A LONG CYLINDER AND ROLL UP. PINCH SEAM TOGETHER AND PLACE SEAM SIDE DOWN ON PARCHMENT-LINED BAKING SHEET.

MAKE THREE SMALL CUTS IN THE TOP OF THE ROLL TO MAKE THREE LARGE ROLLS OR ALTERNATIVELY MAKE CUTS EVERY 2 INCHES (5 CM) FOR SMALLER ROLLS. BAKE FOR ABOUT 15 MINUTES OR UNTIL GOLDEN BROWN AND PUFFED. CUT TO SERVE. SERVES 2 TO 3 AS A MAIN OR 6 AS AN APPETIZER.

TIP: YOU CAN PURCHASE FROZEN PUFF PASTRY IN A BLOCK OR PRE-REROLLED SHEETS. FOR THIS RECIPE YOU WILL NEED HALF THE PACKAGE. BE SURE TO LET THE PUFF PASTRY THAW IN THE REFRIGERATOR FOR BEST RESULTS. IF YOU DO NOT NEED THE OTHER HALF OF THE PASTRY RIGHT AWAY, KEEP IT FROZEN. OR DOUBLE UP THE RECIPE AND FREEZE THE BAKED ROLLS TO ENJOY LATER!

TRIED TO BORROW SOME BREAD FROM MY NEIGHBOR,
BUT SHE SAID SHE HAD NAAN.

JERK CHICKEN AND SWEET POTATO SHEET-PAN SUPPER

JERK SEASONING IS AN EASY WAY TO ADD FLAVOR TO ANY PROTEIN. HERE IT IS PAIRED UP WITH CLASSIC CHICKEN FOR AN EASY SHEET-PAN SUPPER.

4	CHICKEN LEGS, CUT INTO THIGHS AND DRUMSTICKS (ABOUT 2 LBS/1 KG)	4
1/2 CUP	JERK SEASONING SAUCE OR PASTE	125 ML
2	SMALL SWEET POTATOES, SCRUBBED	2
1	ONION, CUT INTO THIN WEDGES	1
1 TBSP	CANOLA OIL	15 ML
2 TSP	CHOPPED FRESH THYME (OR 3/4 TSP/3 ML DRIED)	10 ML
1/4 TSP	EACH SALT AND BLACK PEPPER	1 ML

PREHEAT OVEN TO 400°F (200°C). PIERCE CHICKEN PIECES ALL OVER WITH FORK. TOSS WITH JERK SAUCE AND PLACE ON PARCHMENT-LINED BAKING SHEET. ROAST FOR 15 MINUTES.

MEANWHILE, CUT SWEET POTATOES INTO FRIES 1 INCH (2.5 CM) WIDE AND PLACE IN A LARGE BOWL. ADD ONION, OIL, THYME, SALT AND PEPPER AND TOSS WELL TO COAT. ADD TO BAKING SHEET AND ROAST FOR ANOTHER 25 MINUTES OR UNTIL CHICKEN IS NO LONGER PINK AND SWEET POTATOES ARE TENDER. SERVES 4 TO 6.

PECAN TURKEY CUTLETS

THE ADDED CRUNCH OF PECANS MAKES
THESE EASY-TO-PREPARE CUTLETS DELICIOUS.
TRY OTHER NUTS TO CHANGE UP THE FLAVOR
AND TEXTURE OF THE CUTLETS.

2	LARGE EGGS	2
1 TBSP	DIJON MUSTARD	15 ML
1 CUP	FINELY CHOPPED PECANS	250 ML
2 TBSP	CHOPPED FRESH PARSLEY	30 ML
$\frac{1}{2}$ TSP	EACH SALT AND BLACK PEPPER	2 ML
1 LB	TURKEY BREAST CUTLETS/SCALLOPINE	500 G
$\frac{1}{4}$ CUP	CANOLA OIL	60 ML

IN A SHALLOW BOWL, WHISK TOGETHER EGGS AND
MUSTARD; SET ASIDE. IN ANOTHER SHALLOW BOWL,
STIR TOGETHER PECANS AND PARSLEY; SET ASIDE.

SPRINKLE SALT AND PEPPER ALL OVER TURKEY
CUTLETS. DIP EACH CUTLET INTO EGG MIXTURE AND THEN
INTO PECAN MIXTURE TO COAT EVENLY, THEN PLACE ON
BAKING SHEET. REPEAT WITH REMAINING INGREDIENTS.

IN A LARGE NONSTICK SKILLET, HEAT HALF OF THE
OIL OVER MEDIUM-HIGH HEAT. COOK TURKEY IN BATCHES,
TURNING ONCE FOR ABOUT 2 MINUTES PER SIDE OR UNTIL
NO LONGER PINK INSIDE. ADD OIL AS NECESSARY WHILE
COOKING. SERVES 4 TO 6.

TIP: TURKEY BREAST SCALLOPINE ARE THINLY SLICED
CUTLETS FROM THE TURKEY BREAST ONLY. IF YOU NEED
TO MAKE YOUR OWN, SLICE THE TURKEY BREAST AS THIN
AS YOU CAN AND, IF NEEDED, POUND TO A THIN $\frac{1}{4}$-INCH
(5 MM) CUTLET.

TURKEY GNOCCHI BAKE

TENDER POTATO DUMPLINGS ARE TOSSED WITH A TURKEY PASTA SAUCE FOR AN EASY FAMILY DINNER!

1 TBSP	CANOLA OIL	15 ML
1 LB	GROUND TURKEY	500 G
1/2 TSP	EACH SALT AND BLACK PEPPER, DIVIDED	2 ML
1/4 CUP	CHOPPED FRESH BASIL, DIVIDED	60 ML
1	JAR (2 3/4 CUPS/700 ML) TOMATO BASIL PASTA SAUCE, OR SEE PASTA SAUCE (PAGE 207)	1
1	BAG (2 LBS/1 KG) FROZEN GNOCCHI	1
1 CUP	SHREDDED ITALIAN BLEND CHEESE, DIVIDED	250 ML

IN A LARGE SKILLET, HEAT OIL OVER MEDIUM-HIGH HEAT. COOK TURKEY, WITH HALF EACH OF THE SALT AND PEPPER, STIRRING UNTIL NO LONGER PINK. REMOVE FROM HEAT AND STIR IN HALF OF THE BASIL, PASTA SAUCE AND REMAINING SALT AND PEPPER; SET ASIDE. PREHEAT OVEN TO 400°F (200°C).

IN A LARGE POT OF BOILING SALTED WATER, COOK GNOCCHI FOR 8 MINUTES OR UNTIL THEY FLOAT TO THE TOP AND ARE TENDER THROUGHOUT. DRAIN WELL AND TOSS WITH SAUCE AND HALF OF THE CHEESE. SPOON INTO CASSEROLE DISH AND SPRINKLE WITH REMAINING CHEESE AND BASIL. BAKE FOR 10 MINUTES OR UNTIL CHEESE IS MELTED. SERVES 4 TO 6.

PORK AND LAMB

BACON PARMESAN POPOVERS

IT'S HARD TO STOP AT JUST ONE FLUFFY, SLIGHTLY CUSTARDY POPOVER WITH BACON AND PARMESAN. THESE ARE BAKED IN A MUFFIN TIN SO YOU DON'T NEED A SPECIAL POPOVER PAN.

8	STRIPS BACON, CHOPPED INTO $1/2$-INCH (1 CM) PIECES	8
	CANOLA OIL	
4	LARGE EGGS	4
1 CUP	2% MILK	250 ML
1 CUP	ALL-PURPOSE FLOUR	250 ML
$1/4$ TSP	EACH SALT AND BLACK PEPPER	1 ML
$1/4$ CUP	GRATED PARMESAN CHEESE	60 ML

IN A SKILLET, COOK BACON UNTIL CHEWY AND TENDER. TRANSFER BACON TO A PAPER TOWEL-LINED PLATE, THEN POUR BACON FAT INTO A SMALL HEATPROOF MEASURING CUP AND ADD ENOUGH CANOLA OIL TO MEASURE $1/4$ CUP (60 ML); SET ASIDE. IN A LARGE BOWL, WHISK EGGS, THEN WHISK IN MILK. ADD FLOUR, SALT, PEPPER AND CHEESE AND WHISK UNTIL SMOOTH; LET REST FOR 30 MINUTES ON THE COUNTER. MEANWHILE, MOVE OVEN RACK TO THE BOTTOM THIRD.

PREHEAT OVEN TO 450°F (230°C) AND PLACE A 12-CUP MUFFIN PAN ON A BAKING TRAY (TO CATCH ANY OIL OR BATTER DRIPS) AND PLACE THEM IN OVEN TO HEAT.

ONCE OVEN IS HEATED, REMOVE THE HOT MUFFIN PAN AND TRAY FROM OVEN AND POUR 1 TSP (5 ML) BACON FAT/CANOLA OIL MIXTURE INTO EACH CUP. EVENLY DIVIDE BACON PIECES INTO EACH CUP, THEN RETURN PAN AND TRAY TO OVEN TO HEAT FOR 2 MINUTES, UNTIL IT IS VERY HOT.

WORKING QUICKLY, REMOVE THE MUFFIN PAN AND TRAY FROM THE OVEN. GIVE THE BATTER A QUICK STIR, THEN, USING A LADLE, EVENLY DISTRIBUTE THE BATTER AMONG THE CUPS, ABOUT $\frac{1}{4}$ CUP (60 ML) EACH. RETURN PAN AND TRAY TO OVEN AND BAKE FOR 20 TO 25 MINUTES OR UNTIL PUFFED AND GOLDEN BROWN. DO NOT OPEN THE OVEN DOOR DURING BAKING TIME. REMOVE FROM OVEN AND SERVE RIGHT AWAY. MAKES 12.

TIP: TO REHEAT, PLACE POPOVERS IN A PREHEATED OVEN, SET TO 350°F (180°C). BAKE FOR 5 MINUTES, OR JUST UNTIL THEY ARE WARM AND CRISP.

DON'T GO BACON MY HEART... I COULDN'T IF I FRIED.

SAVORY GRILLED PORK TENDERLOIN

IT DOESN'T TAKE LONG TO COOK UP THIS JUICY FLAVORFUL GRILLED PORK. IT'S OKAY IF THE COOKED PORK IS SLIGHTLY PINK IN THE CENTER, BUT MAKE SURE TO USE A THERMOMETER TO CHECK FOR DONENESS.

1/3 CUP	SOY SAUCE	75 ML
2 TBSP	PACKED BROWN SUGAR	30 ML
5	GARLIC CLOVES, MINCED	5
2 TSP	GROUND CUMIN	10 ML
1/2 TSP	BLACK PEPPER	2 ML
2 TBSP	CANOLA OIL	30 ML
2 LBS	PORK TENDERLOIN (ABOUT 2)	1 KG

IN A RESEALABLE PLASTIC BAG, COMBINE SOY SAUCE, BROWN SUGAR, GARLIC, CUMIN, PEPPER AND OIL. ADD PORK, TURNING TO COAT, REFRIGERATE 1 HOUR OR OVERNIGHT, TURNING PORK OCCASIONALLY.

PREHEAT BARBECUE GRILL TO HIGH. REMOVE MEAT FROM MARINADE, DISCARDING MARINADE. GRILL FOR 10 TO 15 MINUTES, TURNING EVERY FEW MINUTES, OR UNTIL A MEAT THERMOMETER INSERTED IN THE THICKEST PART OF THE MEAT REGISTERS 145°F (63°C) OR TO DESIRED DONENESS. SERVES 8.

TIP: YOU CAN FREEZE THE FRESH PORK TENDERLOIN IN THE MARINADE FOR UP TO 3 MONTHS. THAW OVERNIGHT IN THE REFRIGERATOR, THEN GRILL AS DIRECTED.

NICOLAS'S ITALIAN-STYLE PORK CHOPS

NEED A QUICK WEEKNIGHT MEAL? THIS IS ONE THAT PLAYS ON REPEAT IN EMILY'S HOUSE BECAUSE HER SON NICOLAS IS A HUGE FAN OF THE BREADING. IT'S ALWAYS HELPFUL TO GET THE KIDS COOKING EARLY — YOUR FAMILY WILL BENEFIT! SERVE UP ALONGSIDE A CRISP GREEN SALAD OR YOUR FAVORITE ROAST POTATO RECIPE.

4	BONELESS PORK LOIN CHOPS	4
1/2 TSP	EACH SALT AND BLACK PEPPER	2 ML
1	LARGE EGG	1
1/4 CUP	DRY SEASONED BREAD CRUMBS	60 ML
1/4 CUP	GRATED PARMESAN CHEESE	60 ML
2 TBSP	CANOLA OIL	30 ML
4	LEMON WEDGES	4

SPRINKLE PORK CHOPS WITH SALT AND PEPPER. IN A SHALLOW BOWL, BEAT EGG LIGHTLY; SET ASIDE. IN ANOTHER SHALLOW BOWL, STIR TOGETHER BREAD CRUMBS, CHEESE AND OIL. PREHEAT OVEN TO 425°F (220°C).

DIP PORK CHOPS IN EGG TO COAT, LETTING EXCESS DRIP OFF. COAT BOTH SIDES WELL IN BREAD CRUMB MIXTURE AND PLACE ON PARCHMENT PAPER-LINED BAKING SHEET. REPEAT WITH ALL PORK CHOPS. ROAST IN OVEN FOR 10 MINUTES OR UNTIL GOLDEN AND HINT OF PINK REMAINS INSIDE. SERVE WITH LEMON WEDGES TO SQUEEZE OVER TOP. SERVES 4.

HAM AND RICOTTA-STUFFED LASAGNA ROLLS

ROLLED LASAGNA NOODLES ARE FILLED WITH TWO KINDS OF CHEESE AND HAM. YOU CAN USE STORE-BOUGHT PASTA SAUCE OR TRY OUR TASTY HOMEMADE PASTA SAUCE ON PAGE 207.

2½ CUPS	PASTA SAUCE	625 ML
2 CUPS	RICOTTA	500 ML
2 CUPS	COOKED FINELY CHOPPED HAM	500 ML
1 CUP	GRATED PARMESAN CHEESE, DIVIDED	250 ML
½ TSP	BLACK PEPPER	2 ML
12	LASAGNA NOODLES	12

PREHEAT OVEN TO 375°F (190°C). SET ASIDE A GREASED 13 BY 9-INCH (33 BY 23 CM) CASSEROLE DISH. SPREAD 1 CUP (250 ML) OF THE PASTA SAUCE OVER THE BOTTOM OF THE DISH. IN A BOWL, COMBINE RICOTTA, HAM, ¾ CUP (175 ML) CHEESE AND PEPPER. IN A LARGE POT OF SALTED BOILING WATER, COOK LASAGNA NOODLES FOR ABOUT 6 MINUTES OR UNTIL AL DENTE; DRAIN WELL.

ON A LIGHTLY OILED BAKING SHEET, LAY OUT COOKED LASAGNA NOODLES AND EVENLY DIVIDE CHEESE AND HAM MIXTURE ALONG THE LENGTH OF THE NOODLES. ROLL UP PASTA JELLY-ROLL STYLE AND PLACE SEAM SIDE DOWN IN DISH. POUR REMAINING PASTA SAUCE ON TOP AND COVER WITH FOIL.

BAKE 30 MINUTES. REMOVE CASSEROLE FROM OVEN AND SET TO BROIL. REMOVE FOIL AND SPRINKLE CASSEROLE WITH REMAINING $\frac{1}{4}$ CUP (60 ML) CHEESE; BROIL FOR 2 TO 3 MINUTES, OR UNTIL CHEESE IS LIGHT GOLDEN BROWN. MAKES 12 ROLLS.

MAKE AHEAD: ASSEMBLE LASAGNA ROLLS, THEN COVER AND REFRIGERATE FOR 1 DAY. REMOVE FROM REFRIGERATOR 30 MINUTES BEFORE BAKING. BAKE AS DIRECTED.

WHAT DO YOU CALL A FAKE NOODLE?
AN IMPASTA!

ROASTED CAULIFLOWER AND CHORIZO GNOCCHI

THIS CHUNKY SAUCE IS PERFECT FOR ENJOYING A VARIATION OF TEXTURE AND FLAVOR IN EACH BITE. YOU NEVER KNOW IF YOU WILL END UP WITH MORE CHORIZO OR CAULIFLOWER.

1	HEAD CAULIFLOWER, CUT INTO SMALL FLORETS	1
3 TBSP	EXTRA VIRGIN OLIVE OIL, DIVIDED	45 ML
1/4 TSP	EACH SALT AND BLACK PEPPER	1 ML
1	PACKAGE (8 OZ/250 G) SEMI-DRIED MILD CHORIZO SAUSAGE, CHOPPED	1
1/2 CUP	BEEF OR CHICKEN BROTH	125 ML
1	PACKAGE (1 LB/500 G) GNOCCHI (FRESH OR FROZEN)	1
3 TBSP	BUTTER	45 ML

PREHEAT OVEN TO 400°F (200°C). IN A LARGE BOWL, TOSS CAULIFLOWER FLORETS WITH 2 TBSP (30 ML) OF THE OIL, SALT AND PEPPER. SPREAD OVER PARCHMENT PAPER-LINED BAKING SHEET AND ROAST IN 400°F (200°C) OVEN FOR ABOUT 35 MINUTES OR UNTIL GOLDEN BROWN AND TENDER CRISP. SET ASIDE. (YOU CAN DO THIS THE NIGHT BEFORE FOR A QUICK WEEKNIGHT MEAL THE NEXT DAY! SIMPLY STORE COVERED IN REFRIGERATOR.)

IN A LARGE DEEP NONSTICK SKILLET, HEAT REMAINING OIL OVER MEDIUM HEAT AND SAUTÉ SAUSAGE FOR ABOUT 8 MINUTES OR UNTIL STARTING TO BECOME GOLDEN. STIR IN BROTH; KEEP WARM.

MEANWHILE, IN A POT OF BOILING SALTED WATER, COOK GNOCCHI FOR ABOUT 5 MINUTES OR UNTIL THEY FLOAT TO THE TOP AND ARE TENDER BUT FIRM. USING A SLOTTED SPOON OR SMALL SIEVE, LIFT GNOCCHI OUT OF WATER AND ADD TO SKILLET WITH SAUSAGE. ADD BUTTER AND COOK OVER LOW HEAT. STIR IN ROASTED CAULIFLOWER AND TOSS TO COMBINE UNTIL HEATED THROUGH. SERVE IN SHALLOW BOWLS. SERVES 4 TO 6.

SAUSAGE TURNOVERS

PUFF PASTRY IS FAVORITE STAPLE INGREDIENT IN OUR FREEZERS. THESE GOLDEN PUFFED TRIANGLES SURROUNDING A SWEET AND GARLICKY SAUSAGE FILLING WILL BE LOVE AT FIRST BITE. SYLVIA SHARED THESE WITH HER NEIGHBORS AND THEY ASKED FOR SECONDS!

I TBSP	CANOLA OIL	15 ML
I	ONION, FINELY CHOPPED	I
I LB	FRESH HONEY GARLIC PORK SAUSAGE, CASINGS REMOVED	500 G
3 TBSP	MANGO CHUTNEY	45 ML
I TSP	BLACK PEPPER	5 ML
I LB	FROZEN PUFF PASTRY, THAWED	500 G
I	LARGE EGG	I

IN A LARGE SKILLET, HEAT OIL OVER MEDIUM-HIGH HEAT. ADD ONIONS AND COOK FOR ABOUT 5 MINUTES, UNTIL LIGHT GOLDEN BROWN. ADD SAUSAGE AND COOK, BREAKING IT UP WITH A SPOON FOR ABOUT 8 MINUTES UNTIL MEAT IS COOKED THROUGH. STIR IN CHUTNEY AND PEPPER. COOL MEAT MIXTURE.

PREHEAT OVEN TO 425°F (220°C). SET ASIDE A PARCHMENT-LINED BAKING SHEET. BEAT EGG WITH I TSP (5 ML) WATER; SET ASIDE. ON A LIGHTLY FLOURED SURFACE, ROLL PASTRY OUT INTO TWO II- BY II-INCH (27.5 BY 27.5 CM) SQUARES. CUT EACH SQUARE INTO FOUR SMALLER SQUARES. BRUSH THE EDGES OF THE SQUARES WITH EGG WASH. DIVIDE SAUSAGE MIXTURE ONTO THE CENTER OF EACH PASTRY SQUARE; FOLD OVER TO FORM

A TRIANGLE. PINCH THE PASTRY EDGES TOGETHER OR PRESS DOWN WITH A FORK TO SEAL THEM. TRANSFER TURNOVERS TO PREPARED BAKING SHEET. BRUSH THE TOP OF THE TURNOVERS WITH THE EGG WASH. WITH A SMALL KNIFE, CUT A FEW VENT HOLES FOR STEAM TO ESCAPE.

BAKE 25 MINUTES OR UNTIL GOLDEN BROWN. SERVE WITH EXTRA MANGO CHUTNEY FOR DIPPING, IF DESIRED. SERVES 8.

TIP: THAW THE PASTRY OVERNIGHT IN THE FRIDGE.

TIP: SERVE WITH EXTRA MANGO CHUTNEY, IF DESIRED.

KETCHUP: IT WAS NICE TO MEAT YOU.
HOT DOG: HOPE TO SEE YOU AGAIN SO WE CAN KETCHUP.

PIZZA PEROGY BAKE

FROZEN PEROGIES ARE ONE OF THOSE INGREDIENTS THAT HELP MAKE MEAL PREPARATION A SNAP. THERE'S NO NEED TO BOIL THEM, AS THE PEROGIES HEAD STRAIGHT TO THE OVEN WITH YOUR FAVORITE PIZZA TOPPINGS.

1	BAG (1.9 LBS/907 G) FROZEN PEROGIES	1
2 CUPS	GRAPE TOMATOES	500 ML
2 TBSP	CANOLA OIL	30 ML
1/4 TSP	BLACK PEPPER	1 ML
12 OZ	PEPPERONI, CUBED	375 G
1/2 CUP	SLICED OLIVES	125 ML
3 CUPS	SHREDDED ITALIAN-STYLE CHEESE BLEND	750 ML

PREHEAT OVEN TO 400°F (200°C). LINE A BAKING SHEET WITH PARCHMENT. IN A LARGE BOWL, COMBINE FROZEN PEROGIES, TOMATOES, OIL AND PEPPER. SPREAD IN A SINGLE LAYER ON PREPARED BAKING SHEET, MAKING SURE THE PEROGIES ARE DIRECTLY TOUCHING THE PARCHMENT FOR MAXIMUM CRISPNESS. SPRINKLE THE PEPPERONI AND OLIVES OVER TOP.

BAKE 30 MINUTES. REMOVE FROM OVEN AND SET OVEN TO BROIL. SPRINKLE CHEESE ON TOP AND RETURN TO OVEN. BROIL 2 MINUTES, OR UNTIL GOLDEN BROWN ON TOP. (WATCH THAT THE PARCHMENT DOESN'T START TO BURN!) SERVES 6.

TIP: IF YOU LIKE YOUR FOOD ON THE SPICY SIDE, SERVE HOT PEPPER FLAKES WITH THIS CASSEROLE.

PROSCIUTTO AND PEA PASTA BAKE

BAKED PASTA DISHES LIKE THIS ONE ARE
A FAVORITE FOR MANY FAMILIES TO ENJOY
TOGETHER. IT'S EASILY PUT TOGETHER AND
SERVED RIGHT OUT OF THE CASSEROLE DISH;
ALL YOU NEED IS SOME GARLIC BREAD ALONGSIDE.

1	PACKAGE (1 LB/500 G) FUSILLI PASTA	1
1/2 CUP	BUTTER	125 ML
8	SLICES PROSCIUTTO, CHOPPED	8
1 CUP	FRESHLY GRATED PARMESAN CHEESE	250 ML
1 1/2 CUPS	FROZEN PEAS, THAWED SLIGHTLY	375 ML

IN A POT OF BOILING SALTED WATER, BOIL PASTA FOR ABOUT 8 MINUTES OR UNTIL AL DENTE. REMOVE 1 CUP (250 ML) OF WATER FROM POT AND RESERVE. DRAIN PASTA AND RETURN PASTA TO POT.

PREHEAT OVEN TO 400°F (200°C). IN A LARGE SKILLET, MELT BUTTER OVER MEDIUM HEAT AND COOK, STIRRING OCCASIONALLY ABOUT 5 MINUTES OR UNTIL BUTTER BEGINS TO BROWN. STIR IN PROSCIUTTO AND SAUTÉ FOR 1 MINUTE. REMOVE FROM HEAT AND STIR IN CHEESE UNTIL MELTED. POUR OVER PASTA WITH PEAS AND ENOUGH WATER TO MOISTEN IF NEEDED. SCRAPE OUT INTO CASSEROLE AND BAKE FOR 15 MINUTES OR UNTIL LIGHT GOLDEN ON TOP. SERVES 4 TO 6.

TIP: NO TIME FOR BAKING? SIMPLY SERVE THE PASTA RIGHT OUT OF THE POT FOR AN EVEN FASTER MEAL.

PULLED PORK PIZZA BRAID

MAKE AN EASY PULLED PORK TO PACK INTO PIZZA DOUGH FOR A DELICIOUS AND DIFFERENT DINNER. SERVE WITH COLESLAW FOR AN ENJOYABLE BACKYARD MEAL.

1	BONELESS PORK SHOULDER ROAST, ABOUT 2 LBS/1 KG	1
1 TBSP	CAJUN SEASONING	15 ML
1/2 TSP	EACH SALT AND BLACK PEPPER	2 ML
1 TBSP	CANOLA OIL	15 ML
1/4 CUP	WATER	60 ML
1	BOTTLE (1 3/4 CUPS/425 ML) BARBECUE SAUCE	1
1 1/2 LBS	PIZZA DOUGH	750 G
1 1/2 CUPS	TEX-MEX OR CHEDDAR MOZZARELLA SHREDDED CHEESE BLEND	375 ML

RUB PORK ROAST ALL OVER WITH SEASONING, SALT AND PEPPER. IN A LARGE SKILLET, HEAT OIL OVER MEDIUM-HIGH HEAT AND BROWN PORK SHOULDER ALL OVER. PLACE BROWNED MEAT IN SLOW COOKER. ADD WATER TO SKILLET AND BRING TO A SIMMER; ADD LIQUID TO SLOW COOKER ALONG WITH BARBECUE SAUCE. COVER AND COOK ON LOW FOR 8 TO 10 HOURS, OR ON HIGH FOR 4 TO 6 HOURS.

USING TWO FORKS OR HEAT-RESISTANT SILICON GLOVES, SHRED PORK AND TOSS WITH SAUCE. LET COOL TO ROOM TEMPERATURE OR OVERNIGHT IN THE REFRIGERATOR.

PREHEAT OVEN TO 400°F (200°C). MEANWHILE, ROLL OUT PIZZA DOUGH ON FLOURED SURFACE INTO A 16- BY 12-INCH (32 BY 24 CM) RECTANGLE. PLACE ON LARGE GREASED OR PARCHMENT PAPER-LINED BAKING SHEET AND RESHAPE. MOUND PORK IN CENTER OF DOUGH, LEAVING A 2-INCH (5 CM) BORDER AT SHORT ENDS AND ABOUT 3 INCHES (7.5 CM) ON LONG ENDS. SPRINKLE CHEESE ALL OVER TOP. CUT DIAGONAL SLASHES ABOUT 1 INCH (2.5 CM) WIDE ALONG BOTH LONG SIDES OF DOUGH. CRISSCROSS STRIPS OVER FILLING TO COVER, TO GET A BRAIDED LOOK.

BAKE FOR ABOUT 15 MINUTES OR UNTIL GOLDEN BROWN. LET COOL SLIGHTLY BEFORE SERVING. SERVES 6 TO 8.

TIP: PACKAGE SIZES OF PIZZA DOUGH VARY, BUT SOMETHING CLOSE TO THIS AMOUNT WILL WORK.

WHAT DID BACON SAY TO TOMATO?
LETTUCE GET TOGETHER.

SAUSAGE POLENTA
OPEN-FACE SLIDERS

SAVORING A BURGER WITHOUT A BUN IS
ALMOST A COMMONPLACE PLEASURE NOWADAYS.
SERVE WITH A SPLASH OF HOT PEPPER
SAUCE FOR ADDED KICK IF YOU LIKE.

I LB	ITALIAN SAUSAGE MEAT OR SAUSAGES, CASINGS REMOVED	500 G
2	GREEN ONIONS, FINELY CHOPPED	2
$\frac{1}{4}$ TSP	EACH SALT AND BLACK PEPPER, DIVIDED	I ML
I	TUBE (2 LBS/I KG) POLENTA	I
I	LOG OR BALL (8 OZ/250 G) FRESH MOZZARELLA OR LARGE BOCCONCINI, SLICED	I
12	FRESH BASIL LEAVES	12

IN A LARGE BOWL, COMBINE SAUSAGE MEAT, ONIONS
AND HALF OF THE SALT AND PEPPER. FORM INTO
12 SMALL PATTIES.

CUT POLENTA INTO 12 CIRCLES. SPRAY LARGE NONSTICK
SKILLET WITH COOKING SPRAY AND PAN-FRY PATTIES, IN
BATCHES IF NECESSARY, OVER MEDIUM-HIGH HEAT FOR
ABOUT 5 MINUTES PER SIDE OR UNTIL GOLDEN BROWN.
REMOVE TO BAKING SHEET.

IN SAME SKILLET, LIGHTLY PAN-FRY POLENTA CIRCLES.
PLACE EACH SLIDER ON POLENTA CIRCLE AND TOP WITH
MOZZARELLA; SPRINKLE WITH SALT AND PEPPER AND
TOP WITH BASIL LEAF. SERVES 4 TO 6.

TIP: YOU CAN ALSO GRILL THE POLENTA CIRCLES AND
SAUSAGES, IF DESIRED, OVER MEDIUM-HIGH HEAT. BRUSH
BOTH THE SAUSAGE PATTIES AND POLENTA WITH OIL
BEFORE GRILLING.

STIR-FRIED PORK AND MUSHROOM LETTUCE CUPS

QUICK AND EASY, THESE ARE PERFECT FOR THE FAMILY TO CREATE TOGETHER. LAY OUT THE LETTUCE CUPS AND THE FILLING SEPARATELY SO EVERYONE CAN CREATE THEIR OWN TO WRAP UP AND ENJOY. OR SERVE IT AS A SALAD ON THE LETTUCE TO EAT WITH A FORK!

1 TBSP	CANOLA OIL	15 ML
2	PACKAGES (8 OZ/227 G EACH) GOURMET MIX SLICED MUSHROOMS	2
14 OZ	GROUND PORK	400 G
4	GARLIC CLOVES, MINCED	4
3/4 TSP	SALT, DIVIDED	3 ML
1/4 TSP	BLACK PEPPER	1 ML
3/4 CUP	SWEET THAI CHILI SAUCE	175 ML
1	HEAD ICEBERG OR BOSTON LEAF LETTUCE	1

IN A LARGE NONSTICK SKILLET, HEAT OIL OVER MEDIUM-HIGH HEAT. COOK MUSHROOMS, 1/2 TSP (2 ML) SALT AND 1/4 TSP (1 ML) OF THE PEPPER FOR ABOUT 12 MINUTES OR UNTIL GOLDEN AND NO LIQUID REMAINS. ADD PORK, GARLIC, PEPPER AND REMAINING SALT AND STIR-FRY FOR ABOUT 5 MINUTES OR UNTIL NO LONGER PINK.

STIR IN CHILI SAUCE AND REMOVE FROM HEAT. BREAK APART LETTUCE AND SERVE PORK MIXTURE IN LETTUCE CUPS. SERVES 4.

TIP: TO CHANGE UP THE FLAVOR OF THE STIR-FRY, USE A DIFFERENT SAUCE FROM YOUR FRIDGE, LIKE HOISIN OR TERIYAKI.

ALE-BRAISED LAMB

LONG SLOW SIMMERS ARE A GREAT WAY TO ADD FLAVOR TO DISHES. THIS WILL HAVE YOUR HOME FULL OF DELICIOUS AROMAS THAT ARE PERFECT FOR A COLD WINTER'S NIGHT AFTER SKIING OR TO CUDDLE IN WITH A BLANKET AND WATCH THE GAME.

1	BONELESS LAMB LEG (ABOUT 2 LBS/1 KG)	1
1 TSP	SALT	5 ML
1/2 TSP	BLACK PEPPER	2 ML
1 TBSP	CANOLA OIL	15 ML
1	LARGE SWEET ONION, THINLY SLICED	1
1	CAN (19 OZ/540 ML) PETITE CUT STEWED TOMATOES	1
1	CAN (12 OZ/355 ML) DARK ALE	1
4	YELLOW-FLESHED POTATOES (ABOUT 1 1/4 LBS/625 G), SCRUBBED AND CUBED	4

CUT LAMB LEG INTO EIGHT EQUAL SIZE PIECES. SPRINKLE LAMB WITH SALT AND PEPPER; SET ASIDE. PREHEAT OVEN TO 350°F (180°C).

IN A LARGE OVENPROOF DUTCH OVEN, HEAT OIL OVER MEDIUM-HIGH HEAT. BROWN LAMB PIECES ALL OVER AND REMOVE TO PLATE. ADD ONION AND SAUTÉ FOR 6 MINUTES OR UNTIL BROWNED. ADD TOMATOES AND ALE; BRING TO A BOIL. RETURN LAMB TO POT WITH POTATOES; STIRRING TO COAT. COVER AND BRAISE FOR ABOUT 2 1/2 HOURS OR UNTIL MEAT IS VERY TENDER. SERVES 6 TO 8.

Turkey Gnocchi Bake (page 110)

Nicolas's Italian-Style Pork Chops (page 115)

Sausage Polenta Open-Face Sliders (page 126)

Salsa Verde Fish Tacos (page 134)

Matthew's Roast Salmon (page 135)

Bow Tie Shrimp and Pesto Pasta (page 138)

Hummus Feta Pepper Pizza (page 155)

Thai Coconut Chickpeas (page 160)

LEMON PARSLEY LAMB CHOPS

FRESH HERBS AND GARLIC MAKE THESE
PERFECTLY TRIMMED LAMB CHOPS TASTY. A
FEW SIMPLE INGREDIENTS WILL TURN THEM
INTO A FAVORITE BACKYARD BARBECUE TREAT.

1/4 CUP	RED WINE VINEGAR	60 ML
2 TBSP	CANOLA OIL	30 ML
4	GARLIC CLOVES, MINCED	4
3 TBSP	CHOPPED FRESH PARSLEY	45 ML
2 TSP	GRATED LEMON ZEST	10 ML
1/2 TSP	SALT	2 ML
1/4 TSP	BLACK PEPPER	1 ML
12	LAMB RIB OR LOIN CHOPS (ABOUT 2 LBS/1 KG)	12

IN A LARGE SHALLOW GLASS DISH, STIR TOGETHER
VINEGAR, OIL, GARLIC, PARSLEY, LEMON ZEST, SALT AND
PEPPER. ADD LAMB CHOPS AND TURN TO COAT. LET STAND
FOR 10 MINUTES.

PREHEAT BARBECUE GRILL TO MEDIUM-HIGH. PLACE
CHOPS ON GRILL AND GRILL, TURNING ONCE FOR ABOUT
10 MINUTES OR UNTIL MEDIUM-RARE OR DESIRED
DONENESS. SPRINKLE WITH MORE SALT, IF DESIRED,
BEFORE SERVING. SERVES 4.

MAKE AHEAD: YOU CAN COVER AND REFRIGERATE THE
MARINATED CHOPS FOR UP TO 8 HOURS BEFORE
GRILLING THEM.

GINGER MAYO MARINATED LAMB

THIS UNIQUE MARINADE DOUBLES AS A TOPPING FOR TWO TIMES THE FLAVOR HIT!

3 TBSP	SEASONED RICE VINEGAR	45 ML
3 TBSP	MAYONNAISE	45 ML
1 TBSP	GRATED FRESH GINGER	15 ML
1 TBSP	CHOPPED FRESH CILANTRO	15 ML
1/4 TSP	EACH SALT AND BLACK PEPPER	1 ML
12	LAMB RIB OR LOIN CHOPS (ABOUT 2 LBS/1 KG)	12

IN A SMALL BOWL, WHISK TOGETHER VINEGAR, MAYONNAISE, GINGER, CILANTRO, SALT AND PEPPER. TOSS LAMB CHOPS WITH 3 TBSP (45 ML) OF THE MIXTURE TO COAT.

PREHEAT GRILL TO MEDIUM-HIGH. PLACE CHOPS ON GRILL AND GRILL, TURNING ONCE FOR ABOUT 10 MINUTES OR UNTIL MEDIUM-RARE OR DESIRED DONENESS. TOSS WITH REMAINING MAYO MIXTURE TO SERVE. SERVES 4.

FISH AND SEAFOOD

CRISPY BAKED FISH STICKS

EMILY'S SONS COULDN'T STOP EATING THESE! WITH ALL THE SPICE AND CRUNCH, THEY KEPT COMING BACK FOR MORE, AND SO WILL YOUR FAMILY. YOU COULD USE OTHER THICK FISH FILLETS INSTEAD OF THE SALMON.

1 LB	CENTER-CUT SALMON FILLET, SKINNED	500 G
1	LARGE EGG WHITE, LIGHTLY BEATEN	1
1 TSP	CHOPPED FRESH THYME (OR 1/2 TSP/ 2 ML DRIED THYME LEAVES)	5 ML
1 CUP	FINELY CRUSHED CORN FLAKES CEREAL	250 ML
2 TSP	CHILI POWDER	10 ML
1/2 TSP	SALT	2 ML
1/4 TSP	BLACK PEPPER	1 ML

CUT SALMON INTO EIGHT EQUAL STRIPS AND SET ASIDE. PREHEAT OVEN TO 425°F (220°C).

IN A SHALLOW DISH, WHISK TOGETHER EGG WHITE AND THYME. IN ANOTHER SHALLOW DISH, STIR TOGETHER CORN FLAKES, CHILI POWDER, SALT AND PEPPER. DIP SALMON IN EGG, LETTING EXCESS DRIP OFF. COAT IN CORN FLAKES MIXTURE AND PLACE ON PARCHMENT PAPER-LINED BAKING SHEET.

BAKE FOR ABOUT 10 MINUTES OR UNTIL GOLDEN AND FISH FLAKES WHEN TESTED WITH FORK. SERVES 4.

TIP: YOU WILL NEED 2 CUPS (500 ML) CORN FLAKES CEREAL TO GET 1 CUP (250 ML) CRUSHED. PLACE THEM IN A RESEALABLE BAG AND USE A ROLLING PIN TO CRUSH THEM OR GET THE KIDS TO HELP AND USE THEIR HANDS TO CRUSH THE FLAKES.

FISH VARIATION: SUBSTITUTE OTHER FIRM FISH LIKE HADDOCK OR COD FOR THE SALMON TO CHANGE UP THE DISH.

IT'S TIME TO CELERYBRATE!

SALSA VERDE FISH TACOS

USING PESTO AS THE HERB STARTER IN THIS SALSA VERDE (WHICH IS MORE OF A SAUCE THAN A SALSA) MAKES IT AN EASY DISH TO COME TOGETHER. AS EMILY'S FRIEND PAOLA SAID, "IT REALLY SURPRISED ME." SERVE A QUICK COLESLAW ALONGSIDE.

1/2 CUP	BASIL PESTO, STORE-BOUGHT, OR SEE BASIL PESTO (PAGE 206)	125 ML
3 TBSP	DRAINED CAPERS, MINCED	45 ML
3 TBSP	RED WINE VINEGAR	45 ML
1/2 TSP	EACH SALT AND BLACK PEPPER	2 ML
1 LB	HADDOCK OR COD FILLETS	500 G
1 TBSP	CANOLA OIL	15 ML
4	HARD TACO SHELLS OR SMALL FLOUR TORTILLAS	4

IN A SMALL BOWL, STIR TOGETHER PESTO, CAPERS AND VINEGAR; SET ASIDE. SPRINKLE SALT AND PEPPER OVER HADDOCK.

IN A LARGE NONSTICK SKILLET, HEAT OIL OVER MEDIUM-HIGH HEAT. ADD FISH AND COOK FOR 4 MINUTES, THEN TURN GENTLY AND COOK ANOTHER 4 MINUTES OR UNTIL FISH FLAKES WHEN TESTED.

DIVIDE FISH AMONG TACO SHELLS AND TOP WITH SALSA VERDE. SERVES 4.

MATTHEW'S ROAST SALMON

WHEN YOUR KIDS HANG OUT IN THE KITCHEN LONG ENOUGH, THEY MIGHT WHIP UP SOMETHING THAT SURPRISES YOU. EMILY'S SON MATTHEW HAS MADE THIS A STAPLE IN HIS COOKING REPERTOIRE.

3 TBSP	MAYONNAISE	45 ML
2 TBSP	GRATED PARMESAN CHEESE	30 ML
1 TBSP	BASIL PESTO, STORE-BOUGHT, OR SEE BASIL PESTO (PAGE 206)	15 ML
1	LARGE GARLIC CLOVE, MINCED	1
4	SALMON FILLETS (ABOUT 6 OZ/175 G EACH)	4
1/2 TSP	EACH SALT AND BLACK PEPPER	2 ML

IN A SMALL BOWL, STIR TOGETHER MAYONNAISE, CHEESE, PESTO AND GARLIC.

PREHEAT OVEN TO 425°F (220°C). LINE A BAKING SHEET WITH PARCHMENT AND PLACE SALMON ON TOP. SPRINKLE WITH SALT AND PEPPER. SPREAD MAYONNAISE MIXTURE ON TOP OF EACH FILLET. ROAST IN OVEN FOR 10 MINUTES, OR UNTIL FISH FLAKES WHEN TESTED. SERVES 4.

SHEET-PAN PROSCIUTTO-WRAPPED SALMON

IF YOU'RE LOOKING FOR A SIMPLE FLAVORFUL DINNER IDEA, THIS ONE-PAN RECIPE IS THE WAY TO GO. LINING THE TRAY WITH FOIL OR PARCHMENT MAKES FOR EASY CLEANUP.

1 LB	ASPARAGUS, TRIMMED AND CUT INTO 2-INCH (5 CM) PIECES	500 G
1	RED BELL PEPPER, SLICED THINLY	1
2 TBSP	CANOLA OIL	30 ML
1/4 TSP	EACH SALT AND BLACK PEPPER	1 ML
4	SALMON FILLETS, SKIN REMOVED (ABOUT 6 OZ/175 G EACH)	4
2 TBSP	BASIL PESTO, STORE-BOUGHT, OR SEE BASIL PESTO (PAGE 206)	30 ML
8	THIN SLICES PROSCIUTTO	8

PREHEAT OVEN TO 425°F (220°C) AND LINE A LARGE BAKING SHEET WITH FOIL OR PARCHMENT. PLACE ASPARAGUS AND RED PEPPER ON ONE SIDE OF THE TRAY AND TOSS WITH OIL, SPRINKLE WITH SALT AND PEPPER. SPREAD BASIL PESTO OVER THE TOP OF EACH FILLET, THEN WRAP EACH WITH TWO SLICES OF PROSCIUTTO AND PLACE ON THE OTHER SIDE OF THE BAKING SHEET.

BAKE FOR ABOUT 15 MINUTES OR UNTIL FISH IS OPAQUE AND FLAKES EASILY WHEN TESTED WITH A FORK, AND PROSCIUTTO IS GOLDEN BROWN AND VEGETABLES ARE TENDER CRISP. SERVES 4.

TIP: WASH AND SLICE THE VEGGIES THE NIGHT BEFORE TO SPEED UP MEAL PREPARATION.

ROAST FISH AND BROCCOLI OVEN SUPPER

WHEN FRIENDS AND FAMILY GET EXCITED ABOUT TRYING OUT A RECIPE, YOU KNOW IT WILL BE A WINNER. THIS WELL-TESTED RECIPE WAS LOVED BY MANY AND WILL BECOME A STAPLE IN MANY HOMES.

3 TBSP	SOY SAUCE	45 ML
I TBSP	SESAME OIL	15 ML
2	GARLIC CLOVES, MINCED	2
1/4 TSP	BLACK PEPPER	I ML
I LB	FISH FILLETS (SUCH AS HADDOCK, SALMON OR COD)	500 G
I	LARGE BUNCH FRESH BROCCOLI	I
2 TBSP	CANOLA OIL	30 ML
1/4 TSP	SALT	I ML

IN A SHALLOW DISH, WHISK TOGETHER SOY SAUCE, OIL, GARLIC AND PEPPER; REMOVE AND RESERVE I TBSP (15 ML). ADD FISH TO DISH AND TURN TO COAT; SET ASIDE.

PREHEAT OVEN TO 425°F (220°C). CUT BROCCOLI TOP INTO 2-INCH (5 CM) LONG FLORETS AND IN HALF LENGTHWISE IF TOO LARGE. PEEL STALK AND CUT INTO SIMILAR SIZE PIECES. TOSS BROCCOLI WITH RESERVED I TBSP (15 ML) OF THE MARINADE, OIL AND SALT. SPREAD ONTO HALF OF PARCHMENT PAPER-LINED BAKING SHEET. ROAST FOR 10 MINUTES.

ADD FISH FILLETS TO OTHER HALF OF BAKING SHEET AND RETURN TO OVEN FOR 10 MINUTES OR UNTIL FISH FLAKES WHEN TESTED WITH FORK AND BROCCOLI IS GOLDEN. SERVES 4.

BOW TIE SHRIMP AND PESTO PASTA

BOW TIE PASTA IS ALSO KNOWN AS FARFALLE, WHICH MEANS BUTTERFLY IN ITALIAN. WE LOVE HOW THE PESTO NESTLES INTO THE PINCHED CENTER OF THE PASTA FOR MORE FLAVOR IN EACH BITE. USING BOTTLED PESTO IS A GREAT SUPERMARKET SHORTCUT.

12 OZ	DRIED BOW TIE PASTA	375 G
2 TBSP	CANOLA OIL, DIVIDED	30 ML
I LB	MEDIUM-SIZE SHRIMP, PEELED AND DEVEINED	500 G
2 CUPS	GRAPE TOMATOES, SLICED IN HALF	500 ML
1/2 CUP	BASIL PESTO, STORE-BOUGHT, OR SEE BASIL PESTO (PAGE 206)	125 ML
	SALT AND BLACK PEPPER	
1/3 CUP	GRATED PARMESAN CHEESE	75 ML

IN A LARGE POT OF BOILING SALTED WATER, COOK PASTA FOR ABOUT 8 MINUTES OR UNTIL AL DENTE. DRAIN, RESERVING I CUP (250 ML) OF PASTA WATER.

IN A NONSTICK SKILLET, OVER MEDIUM-HIGH HEAT, HEAT I TBSP (15 ML) OIL. ADD SHRIMP AND COOK, STIRRING FOR 2 TO 3 MINUTES, UNTIL SHRIMP IS ALMOST COOKED THROUGH AND OPAQUE, TRANSFER TO A PLATE. IN THE SAME SKILLET, HEAT REMAINING I TBSP (15 ML) OIL AND COOK TOMATOES FOR I MINUTE, ADD SHRIMP, PESTO AND PASTA AND TOSS TO COMBINE. SEASON WITH SALT AND PEPPER, IF DESIRED, AND ADD SOME OF THE PASTA WATER IF PASTA IS DRY.

DIVIDE THE PASTA ONTO FOUR PLATES AND SPRINKLE EACH WITH CHEESE. SERVES 4.

TIP: SALTING THE PASTA COOKING WATER SEASONS THE PASTA FOR BETTER FLAVOR.

THIS DISH IS SO DELICIOUS, IT'S PRE-PASTA-ROUS!

HARISSA GRILLED SCALLOPS

HARISSA IS A NORTH AFRICAN HOT CHILI PASTE MADE OF INGREDIENTS THAT ADD A DELICIOUS SMOKINESS TO THIS DISH, INCLUDING RED CHILIES, GARLIC, VINEGAR AND SPICES. IF YOU LIKE YOUR FOOD VERY SPICY, ADD THE FULL AMOUNT OF HARISSA PASTE.

1½ to 2 TBSP	HARISSA PASTE	22 to 30 ML
2 TBSP	EXTRA VIRGIN OLIVE OIL	30 ML
1 TSP	GRANULATED SUGAR	5 ML
1 TSP	GROUND CUMIN	5 ML
½ TSP	EACH SALT AND BLACK PEPPER	2 ML
1 LB	LARGE SCALLOPS, PATTED DRY	500 G
1	SMALL RED ONION, CHOPPED	1

IN A SMALL BOWL, COMBINE HARISSA, OIL, SUGAR, CUMIN, SALT AND PEPPER. ADD SCALLOPS AND ONION AND STIR TO FULLY COAT; LET SIT FOR 15 MINUTES. PREHEAT BARBECUE GRILL TO HIGH. THREAD SCALLOPS AND ONIONS ONTO METAL SKEWERS. GRILL FOR 2 MINUTES PER SIDE OR UNTIL JUST COOKED THROUGH. SERVES 4.

TIP: SCALLOPS GENERALLY COME ONE OF TWO WAYS. WET-PACKED HAVE BEEN TREATED WITH A SOLUTION TO KEEP THEM FRESHER FOR LONGER, AND THESE SCALLOPS TEND TO ABSORB MORE WATER. DRY-PACKED SCALLOPS HAVE BEEN SHIPPED ON ICE WITH NO ADDITIVES. IF YOU PURCHASE WET-PACKED SCALLOPS, BE SURE TO DRAIN THEM WELL ON PAPER TOWELS BEFORE USING.

TIP: IF YOU ARE USING WOODEN SKEWERS, SOAK IN WATER FOR AT LEAST 30 MINUTES, OR OVERNIGHT, BEFORE USING.

TIP: HARISSA CAN BE FOUND IN JARS, TUBES AND CANS IN THE INTERNATIONAL SECTION OF MANY GROCERY STORES. ALSO CHECK YOUR LOCAL MIDDLE EASTERN MARKET FOR A WIDER SELECTION.

STEAMED MUSSELS WITH TOMATOES AND SAUSAGE

BUY MUSSELS THAT ARE TIGHTLY CLOSED OR THAT SNAP SHUT WHEN LIGHTLY TAPPED; THERE SHOULD BE NO FISHY SMELL. THE FLAVORFUL SAUSAGE IN THIS DISH COMPLEMENTS THE TENDER BRINY MUSSELS. THIS IS A FAVORITE MEAL OF SYLVIA'S FAMILY. THEY ENJOY IT SERVED WITH CRUSTY BREAD OR FRENCH FRIES TO SOAK UP THE DELICIOUS BROTH.

1 TBSP	CANOLA OIL	15 ML
1 LB	FRESH SPICY ITALIAN OR CHORIZO SAUSAGE, CASINGS REMOVED	500 G
1	CAN (19 OZ/540 ML) PETITE CUT GARLIC AND OLIVE OIL TOMATOES	1
1½ CUPS	WHITE WINE	375 ML
¼ CUP	BASIL PESTO, STORE-BOUGHT, OR SEE BASIL PESTO (PAGE 206)	60 ML
1½ LBS	BLACK MUSSELS, CLEANED AND DEBEARDED	750 G
	SALT AND BLACK PEPPER	

IN A LARGE HEAVY POT, HEAT OIL OVER MEDIUM-HIGH HEAT. ADD SAUSAGE AND BREAK APART INTO BITE-SIZE PIECES. COOK FOR 5 MINUTES UNTIL GOLDEN BROWN. ADD TOMATOES AND WINE AND BRING TO A BOIL, COOK FOR 5 MINUTES. STIR IN PESTO AND MUSSELS, COVER AND REDUCE HEAT TO MEDIUM. COOK FOR 3 MINUTES, OR UNTIL MUSSELS OPEN. SEASON TO TASTE WITH SALT AND PEPPER.

DISCARD ANY MUSSELS THAT HAVEN'T OPENED.
SERVES 4.

TIP: MUSSELS ARE ALIVE WHEN YOU BUY THEM. IT'S BEST TO COOK THEM SOON AFTER PURCHASE; HOWEVER, THEY CAN BE STORED IN THE REFRIGERATOR FOR UP TO 2 DAYS. PLACE MUSSELS IN A LARGE BOWL AND COVER THEM WITH A DAMP TOWEL TO KEEP THEM MOIST.

TIP: DEBEARDING IS REMOVING THE HAIRY PART ON THE MUSSEL — SIMPLY PULL IT OFF TOWARD THE HINGE, THEN GIVE THE MUSSELS A GENTLE SCRUB UNDER COLD RUNNING WATER.

ALL I ASK IS A CHANCE TO PROVE THAT
MONEY CAN'T MAKE ME HAPPY.

PORCINI-DUSTED FISH WITH BROWN BUTTER SAUCE

DRIED MUSHROOMS OFFER UP A DELICIOUS WOODSY FLAVOR TO FISH, AND THE BROWN BUTTER SAUCE TAKES THE EXPERIENCE OVER THE TOP IN TASTE. YOU WILL FIND DRIED MUSHROOMS IN THE PRODUCE SECTION OF THE GROCERY STORE.

1/2 OZ	DRIED WILD MUSHROOMS, SUCH AS PORCINI OR CHANTERELLE	15 G
1 TBSP	FINELY CHOPPED FRESH CILANTRO	15 ML
1 TSP	CHOPPED FRESH THYME	5 ML
1 1/2 LBS	FRESH FISH FILLETS, SUCH AS PICKEREL, COD OR TROUT	750 G
1/2 TSP	SALT	2 ML
1/4 CUP	BUTTER, DIVIDED	60 ML

IN A CLEAN COFFEE OR SPICE GRINDER, GRIND DRIED MUSHROOMS UNTIL THEY ARE A FINE POWDER. PLACE IN SMALL BOWL AND ADD CILANTRO AND THYME; SET ASIDE. USING SHARP KNIFE, CUT FISH INTO FOUR EQUAL PORTIONS IF FILLETS ARE LARGE. COAT EACH PIECE WITH MUSHROOM MIXTURE AND PLACE IN BAKING DISH. COVER AND REFRIGERATE FOR UP TO 4 HOURS.

PREHEAT OVEN TO 425°F (220°C). SPRINKLE FISH WITH SALT. IN A NONSTICK SKILLET, MELT 2 TBSP (25 ML) OF THE BUTTER OVER MEDIUM-HIGH HEAT UNTIL JUST STARTING TO BROWN. ADD FISH, SKIN SIDE DOWN IF IT HAS ANY, AND COOK FOR 3 MINUTES.

TRANSFER TO BAKING SHEET AND ROAST FOR ABOUT 8 MINUTES OR UNTIL FISH IS OPAQUE AND FLAKES EASILY WHEN TESTED.

RETURN SKILLET TO MEDIUM-HIGH HEAT WITH REMAINING BUTTER AND MELT, STIRRING UNTIL FOAMY. DRIZZLE OVER FISH TO SERVE. SERVES 4.

YA BUTTER BACK OFF, PAL!

GARLIC TOMATO
SEAFOOD RISOTTO

ADDING TOMATOES TO A RISOTTO MAKES A RICH SAUCE BASE FOR THE CREAMY RICE DISH. LOOK FOR FROZEN MIXED SEAFOOD TO KEEP IN YOUR FREEZER SO YOU CAN WHIP THIS UP ANYTIME. NO SPECIAL OCCASION REQUIRED!

6 CUPS	FISH, CHICKEN OR VEGETABLE BROTH	1.5 L
1/4 CUP	EXTRA VIRGIN OLIVE OIL, DIVIDED	60 ML
6	LARGE GARLIC CLOVES, MINCED	6
1 1/2 CUPS	ARBORIO RICE	375 ML
1	CAN (19 OZ/540 ML) ITALIAN STEWED TOMATOES	1
1	BAG (14 OZ/400 G) FROZEN MIXED SEAFOOD, THAWED AND DRAINED	1
PINCH	EACH SALT AND BLACK PEPPER	PINCH

IN A SAUCEPAN, BRING BROTH TO SIMMER; REDUCE HEAT AND KEEP WARM.

IN A LARGE SHALLOW SAUCEPAN, HEAT 2 TBSP (30 ML) OF THE OIL OVER MEDIUM-LOW HEAT AND COOK GARLIC FOR ABOUT 2 MINUTES OR UNTIL SOFTENED. ADD RICE AND STIR TO COAT. ADD TOMATOES, INCREASE HEAT TO MEDIUM AND COOK FOR 5 MINUTES.

ADD A LADLEFUL OF BROTH INTO RICE AND COOK, STIRRING UNTIL ALL THE BROTH IS ABSORBED, THEN CONTINUE TO ADD BROTH A LADLEFUL AT A TIME FOR ABOUT 20 MINUTES OR UNTIL RICE IS AL DENTE.

IN A SMALL SKILLET, HEAT REMAINING OIL OVER MEDIUM-HIGH HEAT AND SAUTÉ SEAFOOD MIXTURE FOR 5 MINUTES OR UNTIL JUST COOKED THROUGH. ADD SALT AND PEPPER AND STIR INTO RICE MIXTURE. TURN OFF HEAT; COVER AND LET STAND FOR 5 MINUTES BEFORE SERVING. SERVES 4.

SHRIMP VARIATION: SUBSTITUTE 1 BAG (1 LB/500 G) FROZEN SHRIMP, PEELED AND THAWED, FOR THE MIXED SEAFOOD.

I THINK MY SOULMATE MIGHT BE CARBS.

GRILLED MUSSELS
WITH MANGO CHUTNEY

GRILLING THE JALAPEÑO PEPPERS SOFTENS
THE FLAVORS BUT YOU STILL GET SOME
HEAT THAT MATCHES WELL WITH THE SWEET
MUSSELS AND CHUTNEY. BE SURE TO SLICE A
BAGUETTE TO SOAK UP ALL THE JUICES TOO.

4	LARGE FRESH JALAPEÑO PEPPERS	4
1/2 CUP	MANGO CHUTNEY	125 ML
2 TBSP	WATER	30 ML
2	GARLIC CLOVES, MINCED	2
2 LBS	FRESH MUSSELS, RINSED	1 KG
1/4 CUP	CHOPPED FRESH CILANTRO OR BASIL	60 ML

PREHEAT GRILL TO MEDIUM-HIGH. PLACE JALAPEÑOS ON
GREASED GRILL, TURNING OCCASIONALLY, FOR ABOUT
8 MINUTES OR UNTIL SOFTENED AND GOLDEN. LET
COOL SLIGHTLY.

GENTLY RUB OFF SKIN FROM JALAPEÑOS AND
REMOVE SEEDS. CHOP JALAPEÑOS AND PLACE IN LARGE
FOIL BAKING PAN. ADD CHUTNEY, WATER AND GARLIC
AND STIR TO COMBINE. STIR IN MUSSELS TO COAT AND
COVER WITH FOIL.

PLACE PAN ON GRILL, CLOSE LID AND COOK ON MEDIUM-
HIGH HEAT FOR ABOUT 10 MINUTES OR UNTIL MUSSELS
ARE OPEN. STIR IN CILANTRO TO SERVE. SERVES 4 TO 6.

VEGETARIAN

CHARD-TOPPED SWEET POTATO BOATS

THIS SPIN ON A STUFFED SWEET POTATO IS SPICY, COLORFUL AND FLAVORFUL, INCLUDING HUMMUS ON THE INSIDE. IF YOU BAKE SOME EXTRA SWEET POTATOES ONE NIGHT, YOU WILL HAVE A HEAD START ON THIS RECIPE.

4	SMALL SWEET POTATOES, SCRUBBED (ABOUT 1¾ LBS/850 G)	4
2 TBSP	CANOLA OIL	30 ML
4	GARLIC CLOVES, MINCED	4
2 TSP	HARISSA PASTE (OR ½ TSP/2 ML HARISSA SPICE)	10 ML
2 CUPS	CHOPPED RED, GREEN OR RAINBOW SWISS CHARD	500 ML
¼ TSP	SALT, DIVIDED	1 ML
½ CUP	HUMMUS	125 ML
PINCH	BLACK PEPPER	PINCH

PREHEAT OVEN TO 400°F (200°C). PLACE SWEET POTATOES IN OVEN FOR ABOUT 45 MINUTES OR UNTIL TENDER; SET ASIDE.

MEANWHILE, HEAT OIL IN NONSTICK SKILLET AND COOK GARLIC AND HARISSA OVER MEDIUM HEAT FOR 30 SECONDS. ADD SWISS CHARD AND COOK FOR 4 MINUTES OR UNTIL CHARD IS WILTED. STIR IN HALF OF THE SALT; SET ASIDE.

CUT EACH POTATO IN HALF AND GENTLY SCOOP OUT SOME OF THE INSIDE, LEAVING A GOOD $\frac{1}{2}$-INCH (1 CM) THICK WALL. MASH WITH A FORK AND STIR IN HUMMUS AND REMAINING SALT AND PEPPER. SPOON BACK INTO SWEET POTATOES AND TOP WITH GREENS TO SERVE. SERVES 4.

TIP: IF YOUR SWEET POTATOES ARE LARGE, USE ONLY TWO.

TATERS GONNA TATE.

MUSHROOM RISOTTO

HERE THIS CLASSIC CREAMY RICE DISH IS
HEIGHTENED BY THE ADDITION OF EXOTIC
MUSHROOMS. TRY A VARIETY OF MUSHROOMS
FOR A DIFFERENT TASTE EACH TIME YOU MAKE IT.

2 TBSP	EXTRA VIRGIN OLIVE OIL	30 ML
1	ONION, FINELY CHOPPED	1
1 1/2 CUPS	ARBORIO RICE	375 ML
6 CUPS	HOT VEGETABLE BROTH	1.5 L
4 CUPS	SLICED EXOTIC MUSHROOMS (SUCH AS SHIITAKE, OYSTER, CHANTERELLE OR ENOKI)	1 L
1/2 CUP	FRESHLY GRATED PARMESAN CHEESE	125 ML

IN A LARGE WIDE SAUCEPAN, HEAT OIL OVER MEDIUM
HEAT. ADD ONION AND COOK, STIRRING FOR ABOUT
5 MINUTES OR UNTIL SOFTENED. ADD RICE; STIR TO COAT
FOR ABOUT 2 MINUTES. INCREASE HEAT TO MEDIUM-
HIGH AND ADD MUSHROOMS. COOK, STIRRING FOR ABOUT
5 MINUTES.

USING LADLE, POUR IN ABOUT 1 CUP (250 ML) OF THE
BROTH; TURN DOWN HEAT TO MEDIUM. COOK, STIRRING
UNTIL MOST OF THE LIQUID IS EVAPORATED. CONTINUE
THIS PROCESS FOR ABOUT 18 MINUTES, USING AS MUCH
OF THE BROTH AS NEEDED AND ADJUSTING HEAT SO
AS TO NOT BOIL RICE. COOK RICE UNTIL TENDER BUT
FIRM, THEN REMOVE FROM HEAT. STIR IN CHEESE UNTIL
MELTED AND SMOOTH. SERVES 4 TO 6.

TIP: IF NO EXOTIC MUSHROOMS ARE AVAILABLE, YOU CAN USE REGULAR WHITE BUTTON OR CREMINI MUSHROOMS INSTEAD. COOK FOR ABOUT 8 MINUTES.

DOUBLE MUSHROOM VARIATION: FOR A DEEPER MUSHROOM FLAVOR, TRY USING DRIED PORCINI MUSHROOMS. SOAK 1 PACKAGE (3 OZ/90 G) DRIED PORCINI MUSHROOMS IN 1 CUP (250 ML) BOILING WATER. LET STAND FOR 15 MINUTES. STRAIN THROUGH COFFEE FILTER, RESERVING LIQUID; RINSE MUSHROOMS. DECREASE STOCK BY 1 CUP (250 ML).

ONE DAY YOU'RE THE BEST THING SINCE SLICED BREAD. THE NEXT, YOU'RE TOAST

MAC 'N' CHEESE GNOCCHI

YOU WILL LOVE EACH BITE OF THESE PLUMP, PILLOWY GNOCCHI IN A SILKY CHEESE SAUCE. THE ADDED BONUS IS THAT THIS ONE-POT RECIPE COOKS UP VERY QUICKLY, SO YOU DON'T HAVE TO WAIT LONG WHEN YOU'RE HUNGRY. THIS IS A GO-TO RECIPE FOR SYLVIA'S SON WHEN HE NEEDS A FAST MEAL.

1	CAN (12 OZ OR 370 ML) EVAPORATED MILK	1
3 CUPS	SHREDDED SHARP (OLD) CHEDDAR CHEESE	750 ML
1 1/2 LBS	FRESH POTATO GNOCCHI	750 G
1/4 CUP	GRATED PARMESAN CHEESE	60 ML
1 TSP	DIJON MUSTARD	5 ML
1/2 TSP	BLACK PEPPER	2 ML

IN A MEDIUM POT, OVER MEDIUM-HIGH HEAT, ADD MILK AND BRING TO A SIMMER. REDUCE HEAT TO MEDIUM AND ADD CHEDDAR, GNOCCHI, PARMESAN, MUSTARD AND PEPPER; STIR UNTIL GNOCCHI IS TENDER AND SAUCE IS SMOOTH AND THICKENED, ABOUT 3 TO 5 MINUTES. SERVES 3.

TIP: TALEGGIO, FONTINA OR JACK CHEESE CAN SUBSTITUTE FOR CHEDDAR CHEESE IN THIS RECIPE.

— HUMMUS FETA PEPPER PIZZA —

THIS PIZZA CAN CHANGE, DEPENDING ON WHAT YOU HAVE IN THE FRIDGE. ANY HUMMUS AND ANY VEGETABLE WILL WORK. FOR A GOOEY PIZZA SLICE, SWAP YOUR FETA CHEESE FOR MOZZARELLA AND DOUBLE UP!

12 OZ	PIZZA DOUGH	375 G
1/2 CUP	RED PEPPER HUMMUS	125 ML
1	SMALL GREEN, YELLOW OR RED BELL PEPPER, THINLY SLICED	1
3/4 CUP	CRUMBLED FETA CHEESE	175 ML
1 TSP	DRIED OREGANO LEAVES	5 ML
1/4 TSP	BLACK PEPPER	1 ML

PREHEAT OVEN TO 425°F (220°C). ROLL OUT DOUGH TO A 12-INCH (30 CM) ROUND. SLIDE DOUGH ONTO A PIZZA PAN OR BAKING SHEET. SPREAD HUMMUS OVER PIZZA DOUGH, LEAVING A 1/2-INCH (2.5 CM) EDGE. SPRINKLE WITH BELL PEPPER, FETA, OREGANO AND PEPPER.

BAKE ON LOWEST RACK FOR ABOUT 12 MINUTES OR UNTIL EDGES ARE GOLDEN AND CRISP. SERVES 4.

TIP: FIND READY-MADE PIZZA DOUGH IN BAGS IN THE COOLER SECTION OF YOUR GROCERY STORE. SOME STORES MAY HAVE DOUGH IN THE FREEZER; YOU WILL HAVE TO BE SURE TO THAW IT IN THE REFRIGERATOR OVERNIGHT BEFORE USING.

LENTIL BOWL

BOOST THE FLAVOR OF SIMPLE INGREDIENTS WITH A ZESTY DRESSING USING ZA'ATAR, A CLASSIC MIDDLE EASTERN SEASONING MIX. LOOK FOR IT IN THE INTERNATIONAL SECTION OF MOST SUPERMARKETS.

3 TBSP	ZA'ATAR SPICE MIX	45 ML
3 TBSP	CANOLA OIL	45 ML
1/4 TSP	EACH SALT AND BLACK PEPPER	1 ML
1	CAN (19 OZ/540 ML) CAN LENTILS, DRAINED AND RINSED (2 CUPS/500 ML)	1
2	AVOCADOS, PEELED AND SLICED	2
2 CUPS	GRAPE TOMATOES, SLICED IN HALF	500 ML
1 CUP	CUBED FETA CHEESE	250 ML

IN A SMALL BOWL, COMBINE ZA'ATAR, OIL, SALT AND PEPPER; SET ASIDE. INTO FOUR BOWLS, DIVIDE AND ARRANGE THE LENTILS, AVOCADO AND TOMATOES; SPRINKLE EACH WITH CHEESE. DRIZZLE EACH BOWL WITH ZA'ATAR DRESSING. SERVE RIGHT AWAY. SERVES 4.

TIP: FRESH PITA BREAD OR PITA CHIPS MAKE A GREAT ADDITION TO THIS SALAD MEAL.

PEOPLE ARE LESS JUDGY WHEN YOU SAY YOU ATE AN AVOCADO SALAD INSTEAD OF A BOWL OF GUACAMOLE

SPAGHETTI AL LIMONE

THIS RECIPE SOUNDS AMAZINGLY DELICIOUS IN ITALIAN; TRANSLATED, IT IS LEMON SPAGHETTI, WHICH MIGHT MAKE YOU THINK IT'S NOT THAT IMPRESSIVE. TRUST US, AND EMILY'S COUSIN AMANDA, WHO MAKES IT ON REPEAT; THIS DISH IS SO CREAMY AND ZESTY WITH LEMON THAT YOU WILL WANT TO SHARE IT WITH FRIENDS — AND START SPEAKING ITALIAN.

I	PACKAGE (I LB/500 G) SPAGHETTI	I
I	LEMON	I
I CUP	HEAVY OR WHIPPING (35%) CREAM	250 ML
1/4 CUP	BUTTER	60 ML
I CUP	FRESHLY GRATED PARMESAN CHEESE	250 ML
	SALT AND BLACK PEPPER	

IN A LARGE POT OF BOILING SALTED WATER, COOK SPAGHETTI FOR ABOUT 9 MINUTES OR UNTIL AL DENTE. REMOVE ABOUT 1/2 CUP (125 ML) OF THE COOKING WATER AND SET ASIDE. DRAIN SPAGHETTI AND RETURN TO POT. COVER WITH LID.

MEANWHILE, USING A VEGETABLE PEELER, REMOVE TWO LONG STRIPS (ABOUT 4 INCHES/10 CM) EACH OF RIND FROM LEMON. PLACE IN SMALL SAUCEPAN WITH CREAM AND BUTTER. BRING TO A GENTLE SIMMER OVER MEDIUM HEAT. CUT LEMON IN HALF AND MEASURE 3 TBSP (45 ML) OF LEMON JUICE. WHISK IN CHEESE AND LEMON JUICE INTO CREAM MIXTURE. REMOVE LEMON STRIPS; TOSS WITH SPAGHETTI AND DRIZZLE IN ENOUGH OF THE RESERVED PASTA WATER TO LOOSEN, IF NECESSARY, AND TOSS WELL. ADD SALT AND PEPPER TO TASTE AND SERVE RIGHT AWAY. SERVES 4 TO 6.

MISO TOFU AND VEGETABLES

WHITE MISO ALSO IS SOMETIMES ALSO LABELED AS SHIRO MISO AND CAN RANGE IN COLOR FROM WHITE TO LIGHT BEIGE. IT HAS A MILD SWEET-SALTY FLAVOR. SERVE THIS DISH WITH RICE OR NOODLES.

1	PACKAGE (12 OZ/375 G) EXTRA FIRM TOFU	1
2 TBSP	CANOLA OIL, DIVIDED	30 ML
4 CUPS	FROZEN STIR-FRY VEGETABLE MIX (ONE THAT INCLUDES ONIONS)	1 L
2 TBSP	WHITE MISO	30 ML
2 TBSP	TERIYAKI SAUCE	30 ML
2 TSP	SESAME OIL	10 ML
	SALT AND BLACK PEPPER	

DRAIN TOFU AND PRESS WITH A CLEAN TOWEL TO REMOVE AS MUCH MOISTURE AS POSSIBLE, THEN CUT INTO $3/4$-INCH (2 CM) CUBES. IN A LARGE SKILLET, HEAT 1 TBSP (15 ML) OIL OVER MEDIUM-HIGH HEAT. ADD TOFU CUBES AND COOK, TURNING OCCASIONALLY FOR 10 MINUTES, OR UNTIL GOLDEN BROWN AND CRISPY. TRANSFER TOFU TO A PLATE.

IN THE SAME SKILLET, ADD REMAINING 1 TBSP (15 ML) OIL AND FROZEN VEGETABLES AND COOK UNTIL TENDER CRISP, STIRRING OCCASIONALLY. ADD MISO, TERIYAKI SAUCE, SESAME OIL AND TOFU AND GENTLY TOSS UNTIL VEGETABLES AND TOFU ARE EVENLY COATED. ADD SALT AND PEPPER TO TASTE. SERVES 3.

TIP: THE EXTRA FIRM TOFU CAN BE SUBSTITUTED WITH FIRM TOFU.

TIP: MISO IS A FERMENTED SOYBEAN PASTE AND CAN BE FOUND IN THE ASIAN FOOD SECTION OF YOUR GROCERY STORE.

YOU MAKE MISO HAPPY.

THAI COCONUT CHICKPEAS

THIS SIMPLE FLAVOR-PACKED MEAL COMES TOGETHER IN MINUTES. ADD AS MUCH CURRY PASTE AS YOU WANT, ACCORDING TO HOW MUCH HEAT YOU CAN HANDLE! SERVE WITH HOT COOKED BASMATI RICE AND LIME WEDGES AND, IF YOU LIKE IT, FRESH CILANTRO.

1 TBSP	CANOLA OIL	15 ML
3	LARGE SHALLOTS, FINELY MINCED	3
1 to 2 TBSP	THAI RED CURRY PASTE	15 to 30 ML
1	CAN (19 OZ/540 ML) CHICKPEAS, DRAINED AND RINSED (2 CUPS/500 ML)	1
1	CAN (14 OZ/400 ML) COCONUT MILK	1
1/2 TSP	SALT	2 ML

IN A SKILLET, HEAT OIL OVER MEDIUM HEAT. ADD SHALLOTS AND COOK 3 MINUTES, STIRRING OCCASIONALLY. STIR IN CURRY PASTE AND COOK 1 MINUTE, THEN ADD CHICKPEAS AND COCONUT MILK. COVER AND COOK 10 MINUTES. SERVES 4.

TIP: THAI RED CURRY USUALLY CONTAINS PLENTY OF INGREDIENTS, INCLUDING RED CHILI PEPPERS, GARLIC, SHALLOTS, GALANGAL, LIME LEAVES AND LEMONGRASS.

Firecracker Noodles (page 162)

Cheddar Drop Biscuits (page 174)

Scorched Honey Garlic Green Beans (page 175)

Cranberry Bacon Brussels Sprouts (page 176)

Spicy Roasted Potato Wedges (page 177)

No-Churn Mango Ice Cream (page 184)

Rustic Open-Face Berry Tart (page 186)

Bittersweet Chocolate Mousse (page 192)

ROASTED RED PEPPER CASHEW PASTA SAUCE

THE CREAMY RICHNESS OF THIS SAUCE COMES FROM THE CASHEWS. IT'S DELICIOUS TOSSED WITH HOT COOKED PASTA.

4	RED BELL PEPPERS, SLICED	4
3 TBSP	CANOLA OIL, DIVIDED	45 ML
1 1/4 CUPS	UNSWEETENED ALMOND MILK	300 ML
1 CUP	RAW CASHEWS	250 ML
2 TBSP	NUTRITIONAL YEAST FLAKES	30 ML
1 TBSP	BASIL PESTO, STORE-BOUGHT, OR SEE BASIL PESTO (PAGE 206)	15 ML
1 TSP	EACH SALT AND BLACK PEPPER	5 ML

PREHEAT OVEN TO 425°F (220°C). PLACE RED PEPPERS ON A PARCHMENT-LINED BAKING SHEET. DRIZZLE WITH 1 TBSP (15 ML) OIL, TOSSING TO FULLY COAT. BAKE FOR ABOUT 25 MINUTES OR UNTIL PEPPERS ARE BEGINNING TO BROWN. REMOVE FROM OVEN AND LET COOL 5 MINUTES.

IN A BLENDER OR FOOD PROCESSOR, ADD PEPPERS, REMAINING 2 TBSP (30 ML) OIL, ALMOND MILK, CASHEWS, YEAST FLAKES, PESTO, SALT AND PEPPER AND PURÉE TO DESIRED CONSISTENCY. MAKES ABOUT 2 CUPS (500 ML). SERVES 4.

TIP: NUTRITIONAL YEAST FLAKES CAN BE FOUND IN THE BULK AISLE OR PACKAGED IN THE HEALTH FOOD SECTION OF THE SUPERMARKET.

FIRECRACKER NOODLES

THESE FEW SIMPLE INGREDIENTS PACK PLENTY OF FLAVOR. DRIED RICE NOODLES ONLY REQUIRE SOAKING IN BOILING WATER TO SOFTEN, AND THEN THEY'RE READY TO BE TOSSED WITH THIS SPICY THAI-STYLE SAUCE. MEDIUM TO WIDE NOODLES WORK BEST IN THIS RECIPE.

4 OZ	DRIED RICE NOODLES	125 G
2 TBSP	CANOLA OIL	30 ML
1	PACKAGE (12 OZ/375 G) FIRM TOFU, WELL DRAINED, CUT INTO 1½-INCH (1 CM) CUBES	1
½ CUP	PEANUT SATAY SAUCE	125 ML
1 TSP	SRIRACHA	5 ML
5	GREEN ONIONS, SLICED	5
½ TSP	EACH SALT AND BLACK PEPPER	2 ML

PLACE NOODLES IN A LARGE BOWL OR POT, COVER WITH BOILING WATER AND STIR OCCASIONALLY TO LOOSEN THE STRANDS. LET STAND FOR 3 MINUTES, OR UNTIL NOODLES HAVE SOFTENED BUT ARE STILL A LITTLE CHEWY. DRAIN WELL AND RINSE WITH COLD WATER TO STOP THEM FROM COOKING ANY FURTHER; SET ASIDE.

MEANWHILE, PAT TOFU DRY WITH A CLEAN TOWEL. IN A LARGE NONSTICK SKILLET OVER MEDIUM-HIGH HEAT, HEAT OIL AND ADD TOFU. FRY FOR ABOUT 5 MINUTES, UNTIL TOFU BEGINS TO GET CRISPY AND BROWN. ADD NOODLES, PEANUT SAUCE, SRIRACHA, GREEN ONIONS, SALT AND PEPPER. GENTLY TOSS TO COMBINE; COOK UNTIL HEATED THROUGH AND NOODLES ARE TENDER, ABOUT 5 MINUTES. SERVES 3.

TIP: THIN DRIED RICE NOODLES WILL SOFTEN FASTER THAN A WIDE OR THICKER NOODLE. WATCH CLOSELY TO MAKE SURE NOODLES DO NOT BECOME MUSHY.

TIP: WHEN PURCHASING DRIED RICE NOODLES, TAKE A MINUTE TO READ THE INGREDIENT LABEL; RICE SHOULD BE THE FIRST INGREDIENT. THE PACKAGE IS OFTEN LABELED AS RICE STICKS AND CAN BE MADE WITH WHITE OR BROWN RICE.

TIP: YOU CAN SUBSTITUTE EXTRA FIRM TOFU FOR FIRM TOFU.

RICOTTA ZUCCHINI PIZZA

*INSPIRED BY EMILY'S FRIEND AMY'S RECIPE,
THIS PIZZA CAME TOGETHER QUICKLY AND IS
PERFECT TO USE UP THOSE SUMMER ZUCCHINI!!*

2 CUPS	THINLY SLICED GREEN AND OR YELLOW ZUCCHINI	500 ML
1/2 TSP	SALT	2 ML
12 OZ	PIZZA DOUGH	375 G
1/2 CUP	RICOTTA CHEESE	125 ML
2 TBSP	CHOPPED FRESH BASIL	30 ML
2 TBSP	EXTRA VIRGIN OLIVE OIL	30 ML
1	GARLIC CLOVE, GRATED	1
PINCH	BLACK PEPPER	PINCH

SPREAD OUT ZUCCHINI SLICES ON LAYERS OF PAPER TOWEL. SPRINKLE EVENLY WITH SALT AND LET STAND FOR 30 MINUTES. BLOT TOPS DRY.

PREHEAT OVEN TO 425°F (220°C). ROLL OUT DOUGH TO A 12-INCH (30 CM) ROUND. SLIDE DOUGH ONTO A PIZZA PAN OR BAKING SHEET. STIR RICOTTA CHEESE AND BASIL TOGETHER AND SPREAD OVER PIZZA DOUGH, LEAVING A 1/2-INCH (2.5 CM) EDGE. ARRANGE ZUCCHINI SLICES OVER RICOTTA IN CONCENTRIC CIRCLES, ALTERNATING COLORS AND STARTING FROM THE OUTER EDGE.

BLEND OIL AND GARLIC AND BRUSH OVER ZUCCHINI SLICES. SPRINKLE WITH PEPPER. BAKE ON LOWEST RACK FOR ABOUT 15 MINUTES OR UNTIL EDGES ARE GOLDEN AND CRISP. SERVES 4.

TIP: USE A MANDOLINE OR CHEF'S KNIFE TO THINLY SLICE ZUCCHINI.

VARIATION: TRY USING YOUR FAVORITE HUMMUS FLAVOR AND SUBSTITUTE IT FOR THE RICOTTA.

DRIED BASIL OPTION: NO FRESH BASIL? NO WORRIES. EMILY'S FRIEND PAOLA ALWAYS HAS SOME DRIED BASIL TO SPRINKLE OVER; USE $1/2$ TSP (2 ML) FOR THIS RECIPE.

WHAT HAPPENS IF YOU EAT YEAST AND SHOE POLISH? EVERY MORNING YOU WILL RISE AND SHINE.

HONEY GARLIC CAULIFLOWER BITES

OUR METHOD OF DIPPING EACH CAULIFLOWER FLORET INTO EGG ENSURES THAT THE CRUMBS STAY ON FOR A CRISPY MOUTHFUL WITH EVERY BITE. YOU CAN SERVE THESE CRISPY BITES WITH GREEK YOGURT AS A DIPPING SAUCE.

1 CUP	PANKO BREAD CRUMBS	250 ML
1 TBSP	CANOLA OIL	15 ML
1/2 TSP	EACH SALT AND BLACK PEPPER	2 ML
1	HEAD CAULIFLOWER (ABOUT 1 1/2 LBS/750 G)	1
2	LARGE EGGS, BEATEN	2
1/2 CUP	HONEY GARLIC SAUCE	125 ML

PREHEAT OVEN TO 425°F (220°C). LINE A LARGE RIMMED BAKING SHEET WITH PARCHMENT PAPER. IN A BOWL, COMBINE PANKO, OIL, SALT AND PEPPER. SPREAD IN A THIN LAYER ON PREPARED BAKING SHEET. BAKE 3 TO 4 MINUTES, STIRRING HALFWAY THROUGH. SET ASIDE TO COOL 5 MINUTES, THEN TRANSFER PANKO TO A BOWL.

CUT CAULIFLOWER INTO 1 1/2-INCH (4 CM) FLORETS. PLACE EGGS IN ANOTHER BOWL AND LIGHTLY BEAT. DIP THE FLORETS INTO THE EGG AND THEN GENTLY PRESS INTO THE PANKO MIXTURE. PLACE FLORETS IN A SINGLE LAYER ON PREPARED BAKING SHEET.

BAKE FOR 25 MINUTES, OR UNTIL CAULIFLOWER IS COOKED AND GOLDEN BROWN. GENTLY BRUSH HONEY GARLIC SAUCE OVER TOP AND SERVE IMMEDIATELY. SERVES 4.

TIP: BAKING AND SEASONING THE PANKO BREAD CRUMBS IS KEY TO MORE FLAVOR, COLOR AND CRUNCH.

TIP: THE TOUGH INNER CORE OF THE CAULIFLOWER CAN BE GRATED OR CHOPPED INTO SMALL PIECES TO BE ADDED TO SOUP OR STIR-FRIES.

VEGETABLE NOODLES AND EGGS

THIS LIGHT SPIN ON PASTA WILL KEEP A SPRING IN YOUR STEP. VEGETABLE NOODLES ARE EASY TO GRAB IN THE PRODUCE AISLE AND MAKE A FAST DINNER. EGGS FOR DINNER? YES! THESE EGGS ARE POACHED SOFTLY TO CREATE A CREAMY ADDITION TO THE DISH.

1/4 CUP	EXTRA VIRGIN OLIVE OIL	60 ML
4	GARLIC CLOVES, MINCED	4
2	PACKAGES (12 OZ/340 G EACH) ZUCCHINI OR BUTTERNUT SQUASH SPIRALS	2
1 TSP	SALT, DIVIDED	5 ML
1 CUP	MEDIUM SALSA	250 ML
1/4 CUP	CHOPPED FRESH CILANTRO	60 ML
4	LARGE EGGS	4
	BLACK PEPPER	

IN A LARGE SKILLET, HEAT OIL OVER MEDIUM HEAT. SAUTÉ GARLIC FOR 1 MINUTE OR UNTIL SOFTENED. ADD VEGGIE NOODLES AND 1/2 TSP (2 ML) OF THE SALT; SAUTÉ FOR 2 MINUTES. STIR IN SALSA AND REMOVE FROM HEAT. TOSS WITH CILANTRO AND DIVIDE AMONG FOUR BOWLS.

MEANWHILE, IN A SAUCEPAN OF SIMMERING WATER, ADD REMAINING SALT. CRACK EGG INTO A SMALL BOWL AND LOWER INTO SIMMERING WATER. REPEAT WITH REMAINING EGGS. COOK GENTLY FOR ABOUT 3 MINUTES OR UNTIL DESIRED DONENESS. REMOVE WITH SLOTTED SPOON AND PLACE ON TOP OF EACH BOWL. SPRINKLE WITH PEPPER, IF DESIRED. SERVES 4.

RAVIOLI IN BALSAMIC CREAM

THIS MAKES AN ELEGANT WEEKNIGHT MEAL BUT ALSO A PERFECT STARTER FOR ENTERTAINING YOUR GUESTS. TRY THE LOVELY DARK SAUCE WITH OTHER FAVORITE STUFFED PASTAS LIKE TORTELLINI OR AGNOLOTTI.

2 TBSP	BUTTER	30 ML
1	SHALLOT, CHOPPED	1
1/4 CUP	BALSAMIC VINEGAR	60 ML
3/4 CUP	HEAVY OR WHIPPING (35%) CREAM	175 ML
1/4 TSP	EACH SALT AND BLACK PEPPER	1 ML
1	PACKAGE (1 LB/500 G) FRESH SQUASH OR CHEESE RAVIOLI	1

IN A SMALL SAUCEPAN, MELT BUTTER OVER MEDIUM HEAT. ADD SHALLOT AND COOK, STIRRING OCCASIONALLY FOR 3 MINUTES OR UNTIL SOFTENED. ADD VINEGAR AND BOIL GENTLY FOR 3 MINUTES. ADD WHIPPING CREAM AND BOIL GENTLY FOR ABOUT 3 MINUTES OR UNTIL SAUCE IS THICK ENOUGH TO COAT THE BACK OF A SPOON. ADD SALT AND PEPPER.

MEANWHILE, IN A LARGE POT OF BOILING SALTED WATER, ADD RAVIOLI AND COOK FOR ABOUT 5 MINUTES OR UNTIL AL DENTE AND IT FLOATS TO THE TOP. USING SLOTTED SPOON, REMOVE RAVIOLI TO PLATTER. POUR SAUCE OVER TOP AND TOSS GENTLY TO COAT. SERVES 4.

EGG AND PASTA FRITTATA

*USING LEFTOVER PASTA FOR A FRITTATA
MAKES A GREAT MEAL EASIER. JUST COOK UP
A BATCH OF SPAGHETTI TO USE FRESH AND
SAVE THE OTHER HALF OF THE PACKAGE FOR
A DIFFERENT FRITTATA LATER IN THE WEEK.*

8 OZ	SPAGHETTI	250 G
1	PACKAGE (5 OZ/ 142 G) BABY SPINACH, ROUGHLY CHOPPED	1
8	LARGE EGGS	8
1/2 CUP	GRATED PARMESAN CHEESE	125 ML
1/2 TSP	EACH SALT AND BLACK PEPPER	2 ML
1	JAR (12 OZ/370 ML) ROASTED RED PEPPERS, DRAINED AND CHOPPED	1
1 TBSP	CANOLA OIL	15 ML

IN A POT OF BOILING SALTED WATER, COOK SPAGHETTI FOR ABOUT 10 MINUTES OR UNTIL AL DENTE. PLACE SPINACH IN COLANDER AND POUR PASTA TO DRAIN OVER TOP. SET ASIDE.

IN A LARGE BOWL, WHISK TOGETHER EGGS WITH CHEESE, SALT AND PEPPER. ADD SPAGHETTI MIXTURE AND ROASTED RED PEPPERS, STIRRING TO COAT AND COMBINE.

IN A LARGE NONSTICK SKILLET, HEAT OIL OVER MEDIUM HEAT. GENTLY POUR SPAGHETTI MIXTURE INTO SKILLET AND SPREAD AROUND IN SKILLET. COOK FOR

ABOUT 10 MINUTES OR UNTIL EDGES AND CENTER ARE SET. PLACE A LARGE PLATE ON TOP OF MIXTURE IN PAN AND CAREFULLY TURN OVER, THEN SLIDE MIXTURE, COOKED SIDE UP, BACK INTO SKILLET. CONTINUE COOKING FOR ABOUT 8 MINUTES OR UNTIL EGG IS COOKED THROUGH AND GOLDEN. CUT INTO WEDGES TO SERVE. SERVES 4 TO 6.

THERE ARE APPROXIMATELY 45 SECONDS BETWEEN "I'LL MAKE US AN OMELET" AND "WE'RE HAVING SCRAMBLED EGGS"!

SUPERFAST EGG AND RICOTTA LASAGNA

MAKE LASAGNA FOR DINNER IN A FLASH WITH THIS GREAT IDEA. NO NEED TO BOIL WATER FOR THIS MEAL; JUST TAKE WONTON WRAPPERS OUT OF THE PACKAGE AND BAKE.

1½ CUPS	CHUNKY VEGETABLE PASTA SAUCE	375 ML
½ CUP	WATER	125 ML
¼ TSP	BLACK PEPPER	1 ML
1	PACKAGE (8 OZ/250 G) WONTON WRAPPERS	1
1	TUB (16 OZ/475 G) RICOTTA OR COTTAGE CHEESE	1
6	HARD-COOKED LARGE EGGS, SLICED	6
2 CUPS	SHREDDED ITALIAN CHEESE BLEND	500 ML

PREHEAT OVEN TO 350°F (180°C). IN A BOWL, COMBINE PASTA SAUCE WITH WATER AND PEPPER. SPREAD ABOUT ½ CUP (125 ML) OF THE SAUCE IN AN 8- BY 8-INCH (20 BY 20 CM) BAKING DISH. COVER BOTTOM WITH WONTON WRAPPERS, OVERLAPPING SLIGHTLY; THEN SPREAD ANOTHER ⅓ CUP (75 ML) OF THE SAUCE. TOP WITH ONE THIRD EACH OF THE RICOTTA AND EGGS. SPRINKLE WITH ½ CUP (125 ML) OF THE CHEESE. REPEAT LAYERS TWICE.

ARRANGE REMAINING WONTON WRAPPERS OVER TOP; SPREAD WITH REMAINING SAUCE AND CHEESE. BAKE FOR ABOUT 30 MINUTES OR UNTIL BUBBLY. LET STAND 5 MINUTES BEFORE CUTTING. SERVES 4.

SIDES

CHEDDAR DROP BISCUITS

THESE FLUFFY AND CHEESY BISCUITS COME TOGETHER IN A FLASH; PLUS THERE'S NO KNEADING OR ROLLING THE DOUGH.

2 CUPS	ALL-PURPOSE FLOUR	500 ML
I TBSP	BAKING POWDER	15 ML
1/2 TSP	EACH SALT AND BLACK PEPPER	2 ML
1/2 CUP	BUTTER	125 ML
I CUP	BUTTERMILK, ROOM TEMPERATURE	250 ML
1 1/2 CUPS	SHREDDED EXTRA SHARP (OLD) CHEDDAR CHEESE	375 ML

PREHEAT OVEN TO 450°F (230°C). LINE A BAKING SHEET WITH PARCHMENT PAPER. IN A LARGE BOWL, COMBINE FLOUR, BAKING POWDER, SALT AND PEPPER. IN A 2-CUP (500 ML) MEASURING CUP, MELT BUTTER AND WHISK IN BUTTERMILK. ADD TO FLOUR MIXTURE AND STIR JUST UNTIL COMBINED. GENTLY STIR IN CHEESE.

SPRAY A 1/4-CUP (60 ML) MEASURING CUP WITH COOKING SPRAY AND USE IT TO LIGHTLY SCOOP AND DROP THE DOUGH ONTO THE PREPARED BAKING SHEET, ABOUT 1 1/2-INCHES (4 CM) APART. BAKE FOR 15 TO 18 MINUTES, OR UNTIL GOLDEN BROWN. MAKES ABOUT 12 BISCUITS.

TIP: USE SMOKED CHEDDAR FOR A VARIATION IN FLAVOR.

CHEESY PUNS CRACK-ER ME UP!

SCORCHED HONEY GARLIC GREEN BEANS

SCORCHING THE BEANS GIVES THIS DISH AN AROMATIC SMOKINESS THAT ADDS GREAT FLAVOR. ADD A DASH OF SRIRACHA OR A SPRINKLE OF HOT PEPPER FLAKES IF YOU LIKE A BIT OF HEAT.

2 TBSP	HONEY GARLIC SAUCE	30 ML
1 TBSP	SOY SAUCE	15 ML
1½ TSP	SESAME OIL	7 ML
¼ TSP	EACH SALT AND BLACK PEPPER	1 ML
1 TBSP	CANOLA OIL	15 ML
1 LB	GREEN BEANS, TRIMMED, PATTED DRY	500 G
3	GARLIC CLOVES, THINLY SLICED	3

IN A SMALL BOWL, COMBINE HONEY GARLIC SAUCE, SOY SAUCE, SESAME OIL, SALT AND PEPPER; SET ASIDE.

IN A LARGE SKILLET, HEAT OIL OVER MEDIUM-HIGH HEAT. ADD GREEN BEANS AND COOK 4 MINUTES WITHOUT STIRRING. STIR AND COOK ABOUT 8 TO 10 MINUTES, UNTIL BEANS ARE MODERATELY CHARRED AND BLISTERED. ADD GARLIC AND COOK, STIRRING FOR 30 SECONDS TO 1 MINUTE, UNTIL GARLIC TURNS LIGHT GOLDEN. REMOVE FROM HEAT AND STIR IN THE HONEY GARLIC MIXTURE. BE CAREFUL AS THIS MAY SPLATTER A LITTLE! SERVES 4.

TIP: THICKER BEANS WILL TAKE LONGER TO COOK THROUGH.

CRANBERRY BACON BRUSSELS SPROUTS

A LITTLE SMOKINESS FROM THE BACON AND SWEETNESS FROM THE CRANBERRIES HELP MAKE THIS HUMBLE VEGETABLE EXTRA DELICIOUS.

2 LBS	BRUSSELS SPROUTS, TRIMMED AND HALVED LENGTHWISE	1 KG
2 TBSP	CANOLA OIL	30 ML
2 TBSP	BALSAMIC VINEGAR	30 ML
1 TSP	GARLIC POWDER	5 ML
1/2 TSP	EACH SALT AND BLACK PEPPER	2 ML
8	STRIPS BACON, CHOPPED INTO 1/2-INCH (1 CM) PIECES	8
1/2 CUP	DRIED CRANBERRIES	125 ML

PREHEAT OVEN TO 425°F (220°C), WITH OVEN RACK PLACED IN UPPER POSITION. LINE A LARGE RIMMED BAKING SHEET WITH FOIL. IN A LARGE BOWL, COMBINE BRUSSELS SPROUTS, OIL, BALSAMIC VINEGAR, GARLIC POWDER, SALT, AND PEPPER. SPREAD BRUSSELS SPROUTS IN A SINGLE LAYER, CUT SIDE DOWN, ON PREPARED BAKING SHEET; SPRINKLE WITH BACON.

BAKE 25 TO 30 MINUTES, SHAKING PAN TO MOVE THE SPROUTS AROUND ABOUT HALFWAY THROUGH BAKING. REMOVE FROM OVEN AND TURN OVEN TO BROIL. BROIL 2 TO 3 MINUTES TO CRISP UP THE BACON AND BRUSSELS SPROUTS. REMOVE FROM OVEN AND STIR IN CRANBERRIES. SERVES 8.

TIP: QUARTER ANY VERY LARGE BRUSSELS SPROUTS TO ENSURE THEY COOK AT THE SAME RATE AS THE SMALLER SPROUTS.

SPICY ROASTED POTATO WEDGES

CRISPY SEASONED POTATOES WITH CREAMY INSIDES ARE HARD TO RESIST. LEAVING THE SKINS ON THE POTATOES SAVES TIME, PLUS ADDS FLAVOR AND TEXTURE. SERVE WITH KETCHUP, MAYONNAISE OR YOUR FAVORITE DIPPING SAUCE. THESE ARE A BIG HIT AROUND SYLVIA'S DINNER TABLE.

2 LBS	RUSSET POTATOES, CUT INTO WEDGES	1 KG
3 TBSP	CANOLA OIL	45 ML
$1\frac{1}{2}$ TSP	SMOKED PAPRIKA	7 ML
1 TSP	GARLIC POWDER	5 ML
1 TSP	DRIED THYME	5 ML
1 TSP	ONION POWDER	5 ML
1 TSP	EACH SALT AND BLACK PEPPER	5 ML

PREHEAT OVEN TO 450°F (230°C). SET ASIDE TWO PARCHMENT-LINED RIMMED BAKING SHEETS. IN A LARGE BOWL, COMBINE POTATOES AND OIL. ADD PAPRIKA, GARLIC POWDER, THYME, ONION POWDER, SALT AND PEPPER; TOSS TO EVENLY COAT.

EVENLY SPREAD THE POTATOES ONTO BAKING SHEETS IN A SINGLE LAYER, CUT SIDE DOWN. BAKE FOR 25 MINUTES. REMOVE PANS FROM OVEN AND FLIP POTATOES OVER, THEN BAKE AN ADDITIONAL 25 MINUTES, OR UNTIL GOLDEN BROWN AND CRISPY. SERVES 4.

TIP: LEFTOVERS CAN BE CHOPPED AND ADDED TO A FRITTATA OR AN OMELET.

CAULI-TOTS

WE'VE ALL ENJOYED SOME FORM OF THE POPULAR MINI POTATO NUGGETS. HERE WE'VE SWITCHED IT UP TO USE CAULIFLOWER INSTEAD. HAND-GRATE THE CAULIFLOWER OR USE THE SHREDDING ATTACHMENT ON A FOOD PROCESSOR.

3 CUPS	GRATED CAULIFLOWER (ABOUT 1/2 HEAD)	750 ML
1 TSP	ONION POWDER	5 ML
1 CUP	SHREDDED CHEDDAR CHEESE	250 ML
1/2 CUP	PANKO BREAD CRUMBS	125 ML
2	LARGE EGGS, LIGHTLY BEATEN	2
1/4 TSP	EACH SALT AND BLACK PEPPER	1 ML

PREHEAT OVEN TO 425°F (220°C). LINE A RIMMED BAKING SHEET WITH PARCHMENT; SET ASIDE. PLACE CAULIFLOWER IN A CLEAN KITCHEN TOWEL AND SQUEEZE OUT AS MUCH LIQUID AS POSSIBLE.

IN A LARGE BOWL, ADD CAULIFLOWER, ONION POWDER, CHEESE, PANKO, EGGS, SALT AND PEPPER; STIR WELL TO FULLY COMBINE. USING A MINI ICE CREAM SCOOP OR A 1 TBSP (15 ML) MEASURING SPOON, FIRMLY PACK AND SCOOP THE MIXTURE ONTO THE PREPARED BAKING SHEET. (IT WILL BE A LITTLE CRUMBLY.)

BAKE FOR 15 TO 18 MINUTES, OR UNTIL GOLDEN BROWN. SERVE WITH YOUR FAVORITE DIPPING SAUCE. MAKES ABOUT 30.

TIP: THESE FREEZE WELL FOR UP TO 1 MONTH. REHEAT IN A 400°F (200°C) OVEN FOR 10 MINUTES OR UNTIL CRISP AND HEATED THROUGH.

TIP: YOU CAN PURCHASE PRE-SHREDDED CAULIFLOWER, OFTEN CALLED CAULIFLOWER RICE, IN SOME GROCERY STORES. LOOK FOR IT IN THE PRODUCE DEPARTMENT.

TIP: THESE ARE GREAT SERVED AS AN APPETIZER OR AS PART OF A MEAL.

WHAT DID THE DORITO CHIP SAY TO THE OTHER DORITO CHIP?
I CAN'T TELL YOU, IT WAS TOO CHEESY.

SPINACH SKILLET SIDE

GINGER AND GARLIC LIVEN UP SPINACH, WHILE THE ADDED KICK OF HOT PEPPER SAUCE ADDS AN ALMOST MELLOW BALANCE. THIS DISH SERVES WELL AS A SIDE DISH FOR MANY MEALS.

1 TBSP	CANOLA OIL	15 ML
2	GARLIC CLOVES, MINCED	2
1 TBSP	MINCED FRESH GINGER	15 ML
1	TUB (10 OZ/300 G) BABY SPINACH	1
1 TBSP	HOISIN SAUCE	15 ML
1/2 TSP	HOT PEPPER SAUCE	2 ML

IN A LARGE NONSTICK SKILLET, HEAT OIL OVER MEDIUM HEAT AND COOK GARLIC AND GINGER, STIRRING FOR ABOUT 2 MINUTES OR UNTIL SOFTENED.

ADD SPINACH, HOISIN AND HOT PEPPER SAUCE AND COOK, STIRRING FOR ABOUT 5 MINUTES OR UNTIL SPINACH IS WILTED. SERVES 4.

TIP: FOR AN EXTRA KICK, ADD MORE HOT PEPPER SAUCE BEFORE SERVING.

MAKE AHEAD: COOK THE SPINACH AND THEN LET IT COOL AND REFRIGERATE FOR UP TO 1 DAY. SIMPLY WARM IT UP IN A SKILLET OR MICROWAVE THE NEXT DAY FOR A MORE INTENSE FLAVOR.

RICE FRITTERS

THESE ARE PERFECT TO SERVE ALONGSIDE ANY FAVORITE DINNER PROTEIN OR SIMPLY ON THEIR OWN AS A SNACK. SERVE THEM AS IS OR WITH OUR EASY PASTA SAUCE (SEE PAGE 207) TO DIP INTO!

2 CUPS	COOKED/LEFTOVER RICE	500 ML
2	LARGE EGGS, LIGHTLY BEATEN	2
3/4 CUP	SHREDDED ASIAGO OR SHARP (OLD) CHEDDAR CHEESE	175 ML
2	GREEN ONIONS, THINLY SLICED	2
3 TBSP	CORNSTARCH	45 ML
1/2 TSP	EACH SALT AND BLACK PEPPER	2 ML
2/3 CUP	CANOLA OIL, DIVIDED	150 ML

IN A LARGE BOWL, STIR TOGETHER RICE, EGGS, CHEESE, ONIONS, CORNSTARCH, SALT AND PEPPER UNTIL WELL COMBINED.

IN A LARGE NONSTICK SKILLET, HEAT HALF OF THE OIL OVER MEDIUM HEAT. USING A 1/4 CUP (60 ML) MEASURING CUP, SCOOP OUT RICE MIXTURE AND PRESS AND FLATTEN TO A PATTY ABOUT 1/2 INCH (1 CM) THICK; ADD TO SKILLET. REPEAT TO ADD A FEW MORE WITHOUT CROWDING THE SKILLET. COOK FOR ABOUT 3 MINUTES OR UNTIL GOLDEN AROUND EDGES. CAREFULLY FLIP OVER AND COOK FOR ABOUT 3 MINUTES OR UNTIL LIGHT GOLDEN BROWN. REMOVE TO PAPER TOWEL-LINED PLATE AND REPEAT WITH REMAINING RICE MIXTURE, ADDING MORE OIL AS NECESSARY. MAKES ABOUT 10 FRITTERS.

POTATO AND RUTABAGA PURÉE

RUTABAGA, OR WAXED TURNIP, IS A WONDERFULLY
TEXTURED VEGETABLE THAT DOESN'T GET USED
ENOUGH. WHEN YOU COMBINE IT WITH POTATOES
IT BECOMES CREAMIER AND EVEN MORE DELICIOUS.
SERVE ALONGSIDE ANY PROTEIN OF YOUR CHOICE
OR ON ITS OWN FOR A BOWL OF COMFORT.

1½ LBS	YELLOW-FLESHED POTATOES, PEELED AND CUBED	750 G
1	RUTABAGA, PEELED AND CHOPPED (ABOUT 2½ LBS/1.2 KG)	1
¾ CUP	HEAVY OR WHIPPING (35%) CREAM	175 ML
⅓ CUP	BUTTER, SOFTENED	75 ML
3 TBSP	CHOPPED FRESH PARSLEY	45 ML
½ TSP	EACH SALT AND BLACK PEPPER	2 ML

PLACE POTATOES AND RUTABAGA IN LARGE POT AND
COVER WITH COLD SALTED WATER. BRING TO A BOIL. BOIL
FOR ABOUT 20 MINUTES OR UNTIL BOTH ARE VERY SOFT.
DRAIN WELL AND RETURN TO POT.

ADD BUTTER AND CREAM TO POT AND, USING ELECTRIC
HAND MIXER, BEAT TOGETHER UNTIL SMOOTH AND FLUFFY.
STIR IN PARSLEY, SALT AND PEPPER. SERVES 6.

TIP: IF YOU DON'T HAVE AN ELECTRIC MIXER, YOU CAN USE
A POTATO MASHER AND MASH UNTIL VERY SMOOTH.

SWEETS

NO-CHURN MANGO ICE CREAM

NO ICE CREAM MAKER IS REQUIRED TO MAKE THIS
RICH AND CREAMY DESSERT. THE CONVENIENCE
OF USING FROZEN MANGO MAKES PREPARING
THIS SWEET TREAT A BREEZE.

3 CUPS	FROZEN MANGO CHUNKS, THAWED	750 ML
1	CAN (14 OZ OR 300 ML) SWEETENED CONDENSED MILK	1
1/4 CUP	FROZEN ORANGE JUICE CONCENTRATE, THAWED	60 ML
2 TSP	VANILLA	10 ML
1/4 TSP	SALT	1 ML
2 CUPS	HEAVY OR WHIPPING (35%) CREAM	500 ML

PLACE AN 8-CUP (2 L) GLASS OR METAL LOAF PAN IN THE
FREEZER. IN A BLENDER OR FOOD PROCESSOR, PLACE
MANGO AND BLEND UNTIL SMOOTH. ADD CONDENSED
MILK, ORANGE JUICE CONCENTRATE, VANILLA AND SALT.
BLEND UNTIL WELL COMBINED.

IN ANOTHER LARGE BOWL, WITH AN ELECTRIC MIXER,
WHIP CREAM UNTIL STIFF PEAKS FORM. GENTLY FOLD IN
HALF THE MANGO MIXTURE INTO WHIPPED CREAM, THEN
FOLD IN REMAINING HALF. STIR GENTLY UNTIL COMBINED.
IT'S OKAY IF A FEW STREAKS OF CREAM REMAIN.

REMOVE LOAF PAN FROM FREEZER. POUR MANGO MIXTURE INTO PAN AND COVER WITH PLASTIC WRAP. FREEZE FOR 8 HOURS OR OVERNIGHT. THIS ICE CREAM MELTS A LITTLE FASTER THAN TRADITIONAL ICE CREAM. SERVE WITH FRESH DICED MANGO, BERRIES AND A SPRIG OF MINT, IF DESIRED. SERVES 8 TO 10.

TIP: A METAL CONTAINER WILL FREEZE THE ICE CREAM FASTER, BUT A GLASS PAN WILL ALSO WORK. FREEZING THE ICE CREAM IN SINGLE-SERVING SIZE CONTAINERS IS ANOTHER OPTION.

NOTHING IS IMPOPSICLE.

RUSTIC OPEN-FACE BERRY TART

THIS FREE-FORM PIE IS SO EASY TO MAKE USING
THE CONVENIENCE OF STORE-BOUGHT PUFF
PASTRY. YOU CAN CHOOSE WHATEVER COMBINATION
OF BERRIES YOU LIKE, SUCH AS BLUEBERRIES,
RASPBERRIES OR CRANBERRIES.

2½ CUPS	MIXED BERRIES	625 ML
¼ CUP	GRANULATED SUGAR, DIVIDED	60 ML
1½ TBSP	CORNSTARCH	22 ML
8 OZ	FROZEN PUFF PASTRY, THAWED	250 G
¼ CUP	SLIVERED ALMONDS, COARSELY CHOPPED	60 ML

PREHEAT OVEN TO 400°F (200°C); ADJUST OVEN RACK
TO LOWER-MIDDLE. SET ASIDE A RIMMED BAKING SHEET.

IN A LARGE BOWL, PLACE ½ CUP (125 ML) OF THE
BERRIES AND GENTLY CRUSH TO RELEASE SOME OF THE
JUICES; STIR IN REMAINING BERRIES. IN A SMALL BOWL,
SET ASIDE 2 TSP (10 ML) OF THE SUGAR FOR SPRINKLING.
IN ANOTHER SMALL BOWL, COMBINE REMAINING SUGAR
AND CORNSTARCH; THEN STIR INTO FRUIT UNTIL EVENLY
COATED; SET ASIDE FOR 5 MINUTES TO ALLOW THE SUGAR
MIXTURE TO ABSORB THE BERRY JUICES.

ON A SHEET OF PARCHMENT PAPER, ROLL OUT PASTRY
INTO AN 11- BY 11-INCH (27.5 BY 27.5 CM) SQUARE. IF
DESIRED, TRIM OFF THE CORNERS TO MAKE A CIRCLE,
OR JUST LEAVE THE CORNERS ON FOR A MORE RUSTIC
LOOK. GENTLY TRANSFER THE PASTRY ALONG WITH
THE PARCHMENT ONTO BAKING SHEET. POUR THE FRUIT

MIXTURE INTO THE CENTER OF THE PASTRY, MOUNDING SLIGHTLY, LEAVING A 2-INCH (5 CM) BORDER. GENTLY FOLD UP THE PASTRY EDGE AROUND THE FILLING, PINCHING AND PLEATING THE PASTRY AROUND THE TART. BRUSH THE OUTER PASTRY EDGE WITH A LITTLE WATER AND SPRINKLE REMAINING 2 TSP (10 ML) SUGAR ONTO THE PASTRY. SPRINKLE NUTS ONTO THE CENTER OF THE TART.

BAKE 40 TO 45 MINUTES, OR UNTIL PASTRY IS GOLDEN BROWN AND THE FRUIT JUICES ARE BUBBLING. LET COOL 10 MINUTES BEFORE SERVING. SERVES 6.

TIP: SERVE WITH WHIPPED CREAM OR ICE CREAM, IF DESIRED.

TIP: FIND READY-TO-USE PUFF PASTRY IN THE FREEZER SECTION. IT USUALLY COMES IN PACKAGES OF AROUND 1 LB (500 G); USE HALF A PACKAGE FOR THIS RECIPE.

TIP: SLICED ALMONDS CAN BE SUBSTITUTED FOR THE SLIVERED ALMONDS.

MAPLE PANNA COTTA

THIS THICK AND CREAMY ITALIAN DESSERT
IS DECADENT AND SIMPLE TO MAKE. WHEN
CHOOSING MAPLE SYRUP, NOTE THAT THE LIGHTER
THE MAPLE SYRUP COLOR, THE MILDER THE FLAVOR.

3½ CUPS	HALF-AND-HALF (10%) CREAM	875 ML
1 TBSP	UNFLAVORED GELATIN (1 ENVELOPE)	15 ML
⅓ CUP	MAPLE SYRUP, PLUS MORE FOR DRIZZLING	75 ML
¼ TSP	SALT	1 ML
1 TSP	VANILLA OR DARK RUM	5 ML
	FRESH BERRIES	

SET EIGHT ½-CUP (125 ML) RAMEKINS OR CUSTARD
CUPS ON A BAKING SHEET. (IF YOU WANT TO UNMOLD
THEM LATER, SPRAY THEM WITH NONSTICK COOKING
SPRAY FIRST.) IN A MEDIUM SAUCEPAN, ADD CREAM AND
SPRINKLE GELATIN OVER TOP. LET STAND 5 MINUTES
TO SOFTEN. PLACE OVER MEDIUM-HIGH HEAT AND
BRING TO A SIMMER, THEN STIR IN ⅓ CUP (75 ML)
MAPLE SYRUP AND SALT UNTIL COMBINED. REMOVE FROM
HEAT AND STIR IN VANILLA. EVENLY DIVIDE MIXTURE INTO
RAMEKINS. REFRIGERATE FOR 3 HOURS OR OVERNIGHT.

TO SERVE, UNMOLD ONTO SMALL PLATES OR ENJOY
FROM THE RAMEKIN. DRIZZLE WITH ADDITIONAL MAPLE
SYRUP AND TOP WITH FRESH BERRIES. SERVES 8.

TIP: PANNA COTTA CAN BE MADE UP TO 3 DAYS IN
ADVANCE. COVER AND STORE IN REFRIGERATOR.

OLIVE OIL CAKE

THIS TENDER CAKE KEEPS MOIST FOR DAYS WITHOUT DRYING OUT. IT'S PERFECTLY DELICIOUS ON ITS OWN OR FANCIED UP WITH FAVORITE TOPPINGS, SUCH AS LEMON CURD WITH WHIPPED CREAM OR SLICED FRESH FRUIT.

1½ CUPS	GRANULATED SUGAR	375 ML
2	LARGE EGGS	2
1 CUP	BUTTERMILK	250 ML
1 CUP	EXTRA VIRGIN OLIVE OIL	250 ML
2 CUPS	SELF-RISING FLOUR	500 ML

PREHEAT OVEN TO 350°F (180°C). LINE THE BOTTOM OF A 9-INCH (23 CM) SPRINGFORM PAN WITH PARCHMENT AND SPRAY THE INTERIOR WITH COOKING SPRAY. IN A LARGE BOWL, USING AN ELECTRIC MIXER, BEAT SUGAR AND EGGS UNTIL PALE AND THICK, ABOUT 1 MINUTE. ADD BUTTERMILK AND OLIVE OIL; BEAT UNTIL COMBINED. GENTLY STIR IN FLOUR, UNTIL JUST COMBINED. POUR INTO PREPARED PAN.

BAKE FOR 45 TO 60 MINUTES UNTIL CAKE IS GOLDEN BROWN OR UNTIL A TESTER INSERTED IN THE CENTER OF THE CAKE COMES OUT CLEAN. LET COOL IN PAN ON A WIRE RACK FOR 15 MINUTES, THEN GENTLY RELEASE COLLAR OF PAN AND COOL CAKE ON A WIRE RACK. SERVES 8 TO 10.

TIP: IF YOU DON'T HAVE SELF-RISING FLOUR, THEN FOLLOW OUR DIY RECIPE ON PAGE 208.

PUMPKIN CHEESECAKE BITES

FASTER AND JUST AS DELICIOUS AS A TRADITIONAL CHEESECAKE. THE CANDY COATING MAKES THESE TREATS EXTRA SPECIAL. BE SURE TO USE CANNED PURE PUMPKIN AND NOT PUMPKIN PIE FILLING. YOU CAN BUY PUMPKIN PIE SPICE MIX OR MAKE YOUR OWN USING OUR RECIPE ON PAGE 209.

8 OZ	BRICK-STYLE CREAM CHEESE, SLIGHTLY SOFTENED	250 G
$\frac{1}{2}$ CUP	PURE PUMPKIN PUREE	125 ML
$1\frac{1}{2}$ CUPS	FINELY CRUSHED GINGERSNAP COOKIES, PLUS EXTRA FOR GARNISHING	375 ML
$1\frac{1}{2}$ TSP	PUMPKIN PIE SPICE	7 ML
PINCH	SALT	PINCH
$2\frac{1}{2}$ CUPS	WHITE CHOCOLATE CANDY COATING WAFERS	625 ML

LINE A BAKING SHEET WITH PARCHMENT PAPER; SET ASIDE. IN A MEDIUM BOWL, ADD CREAM CHEESE, PUMPKIN PUREE, COOKIE CRUMBS, PUMPKIN PIE SPICE AND SALT. STIR UNTIL WELL COMBINED. REFRIGERATE FOR 1 HOUR.

USING A MINI ICE CREAM SCOOP OR TABLESPOON (15 ML), SCOOP UP PUMPKIN MIXTURE AND ROLL INTO BALLS. PLACE ON PREPARED BAKING SHEET AND FREEZE FOR 1 HOUR OR UNTIL FIRM.

ONCE THE BITES ARE FIRM, PLACE CANDY WAFERS IN A HEATPROOF BOWL SET OVER HOT (NOT BOILING) WATER AND STIR UNTIL MELTED AND SMOOTH. GENTLY PUSH IN A TOOTHPICK OR BAMBOO SKEWER INTO A BITE AND DIP ONE AT A TIME TO COAT, ALLOWING EXCESS CANDY COATING TO DRIP OFF. PLACE BACK ON PREPARED BAKING SHEET. SPRINKLE WITH EXTRA COOKIE CRUMBS TO GARNISH.

REFRIGERATE UNTIL COATING IS SET. STORE BITES IN THE REFRIGERATOR UNTIL READY TO SERVE. MAKES 30 BITES.

TIP: PREPARE THESE AHEAD OF TIME AND STORE IN THE FREEZER FOR UP TO 2 WEEKS.

BITTERSWEET CHOCOLATE MOUSSE

SOMETIMES YOU JUST NEED A SIMPLE CHOCOLATEY MOUSSE FOR DESSERT. HERE IS ONE THAT IS RICH AND DELICIOUS WITH A FRESH ZIP OF FRUIT ON TOP TO ADD COLOR AND SWEETNESS.

3	BARS (100 G EACH) 70% BITTERSWEET (DARK) CHOCOLATE, CHOPPED	3
2³/₄ CUPS	HEAVY OR WHIPPING (35%) CREAM, DIVIDED	675 ML
2 TSP	VANILLA	10 ML
2 TBSP	GRANULATED SUGAR	30 ML
3 CUPS	CHOPPED FRESH STRAWBERRIES OR RASPBERRIES	750 ML

PLACE CHOCOLATE IN A HEATPROOF BOWL. IN A SAUCEPAN, BRING 1 CUP (250 ML) OF THE CREAM JUST TO A BOIL. POUR OVER CHOCOLATE AND ADD VANILLA INTO CHOCOLATE. WHISK UNTIL SMOOTH. LET COOL TO ROOM TEMPERATURE, STIRRING OCCASIONALLY, FOR ABOUT 30 MINUTES OR UNTIL SLIGHTLY THICKENED.

IN A LARGE BOWL, WHIP REMAINING CREAM WITH SUGAR; FOLD HALF INTO CHILLED CHOCOLATE MIXTURE. FOLD IN REMAINING WHIPPED CREAM UNTIL WELL COMBINED. SCRAPE INTO PASTRY (PIPING) BAG FITTED WITH STAR TIP, OR USE SPOON. PIPE OR SPOON MOUSSE INTO DESSERT CUPS. SPOON BERRIES OVER TOP TO SERVE. SERVES 6 TO 8.

TIP: YOU CAN MAKE THE MOUSSE UP TO 3 DAYS AHEAD. DO NOT TOP WITH BERRIES UNTIL READY TO SERVE.

TIP: FREEZE THIS MOUSSE FOR UP TO 2 WEEKS, THEN THAW SLIGHTLY IN THE FRIDGE BEFORE SERVING FOR A DELICIOUS SEMIFREDDO DESSERT.

TIP: IF YOU WANT THIS MOUSSE TO BE SWEETER, INCREASE THE SUGAR TO $\frac{1}{4}$ CUP (60 ML) BEFORE WHIPPING WITH THE CREAM.

WHAT KIND OF CANDY IS ALWAYS LATE?
CHOCOLATE

ESPRESSO SHORTBREAD COOKIES

THE SUBTLE FLAVOR OF COFFEE PAIRED WITH CHOCOLATE IS A DELICIOUS VARIATION ON A FAVORITE COOKIE.

1 CUP	COLD BUTTER, CUBED	250 ML
1/2 CUP	PACKED LIGHT BROWN SUGAR	125 ML
2 CUPS	ALL-PURPOSE FLOUR	500 ML
2 1/2 TBSP	FINELY GROUND ESPRESSO COFFEE BEANS	37 ML
1/2 TSP	SALT	2 ML
3 OZ	DARK CHOCOLATE, FINELY CHOPPED	90 G

IN A LARGE BOWL, USING AN ELECTRIC MIXER, COMBINE BUTTER AND BROWN SUGAR; BEAT FOR 3 MINUTES. ADD FLOUR, GROUND BEANS AND SALT AND COMBINE UNTIL MIXED. DIVIDE DOUGH INTO TWO, WRAP EACH IN PLASTIC WRAP AND REFRIGERATE 30 MINUTES.

PREHEAT OVEN TO 325°F (160°C) AND LINE TWO BAKING SHEETS WITH PARCHMENT PAPER. ON A LIGHTLY FLOURED SURFACE, ROLL OUT ONE OF THE PIECES OF DOUGH TO A THICKNESS OF 1/4 INCH (0.5 CM). CUT INTO 2-INCH (5 CM) SHAPES. REPEAT WITH REMAINING DOUGH. TRANSFER TO PREPARED BAKING SHEET AND BAKE 20 MINUTES, JUST UNTIL LIGHT GOLDEN BROWN ON THE EDGES. COOL 5 MINUTES, THEN TRANSFER TO A WIRE RACK TO COOL COMPLETELY.

TO MELT CHOCOLATE, PLACE IN A HEATPROOF BOWL OVER A POT OF SIMMERING WATER; STIR UNTIL SMOOTH. USING A FORK, DRIZZLE CHOCOLATE OVER COOKIES. MAKES ABOUT 50 COOKIES.

TIP: STORE THESE COOKIES LAYERED BETWEEN WAXED OR PARCHMENT PAPER TO PROTECT THE CHOCOLATE DRIZZLE.

YOU'VE BEEN THROUGH A LOT THIS YEAR.
WORDS CANNOT ESPRESSO HOW COOKING CAN HELP.

BROWN SUGAR BERRY TARTS

THESE CREAMY LITTLE TARTS WILL GIVE YOUR GUESTS THE IMPRESSION YOU HAVE BEEN BAKING ALL DAY WHEN REALLY YOU DON'T NEED MUCH TIME IN THE KITCHEN. FROZEN TART SHELLS ARE EASY TO USE AND THE ONLY TRICK YOU NEED TO REMEMBER IS TO REMOVE THEM FROM THEIR LITTLE TINS SO THEY LOOK SOMEWHAT HOMEMADE.

1	PACKAGE FROZEN MINI TART SHELLS (18 TO A PACK)	1
1/4 CUP	PACKED LIGHT BROWN SUGAR	60 ML
1 1/3 CUPS	MASCARPONE CHEESE, SOFTENED	325 ML
1/2 TSP	VANILLA	2 ML
1 CUP	FRESH RASPBERRIES OR SLICED STRAWBERRIES	250 ML

PREHEAT OVEN TO 400°F (200°C). REMOVE TART SHELLS FROM FREEZER AND PLACE ON BAKING SHEET. BAKE FOR ABOUT 10 TO 12 MINUTES OR UNTIL GOLDEN BROWN. LET COOL COMPLETELY.

PRESS BROWN SUGAR THROUGH FINE MESH SIEVE INTO A BOWL. ADD MASCARPONE CHEESE AND VANILLA. USING WOODEN SPOON, STIR TO COMBINE WELL. SCRAPE INTO PASTRY (PIPING) BAG FITTED WITH STAR TIP. PIPE MASCARPONE MIXTURE INTO TART SHELLS TO FILL. TOP WITH RASPBERRIES AND SERVE. MAKES 18 TARTS.

TIP: ALTERNATIVELY, SPOON MASCARPONE MIXTURE INTO SHELLS.

MAKE AHEAD: YOU CAN PREPARE THESE TARTS UP TO 2 DAYS AHEAD. AS THEY SIT IN THE REFRIGERATOR, THE PASTRY DOES SOFTEN.

TIP: IF YOU CAN'T FIND THE MINI TART SHELLS, SIMPLY USE 12 REGULAR-SIZE TART SHELLS AND MAKE THE TARTS A BIT BIGGER.

WHAT'S THE BEST THING TO PUT INTO A PIE?
YOUR TEETH.

CRANBERRY ORANGE BISCOTTI

WHETHER YOU ENJOY THESE WITH COFFEE OR ON THEIR OWN, THEY ARE A SWEET STAPLE TO HAVE ON HAND FOR WHEN FRIENDS COME BY. SOMETIMES YOU MIGHT JUST NEED TO GRAB ONE FOR THE CAR RIDE WHEN PICKING UP THE KIDS.

1 1/2 CUPS	SELF-RISING FLOUR	375 ML
2	LARGE EGGS	2
1/3 CUP	GRANULATED SUGAR	75 ML
1/3 CUP	DRIED CRANBERRIES	75 ML
1/2 TSP	GRATED ORANGE RIND	2 ML

IN A LARGE BOWL, ADD FLOUR AND MAKE A WELL IN CENTER. ADD EGGS AND SUGAR. USING A FORK, WHISK TOGETHER AND GRADUALLY STIR IN FLOUR MIXTURE UNTIL STICKY DOUGH FORMS. STIR IN CRANBERRIES AND ORANGE RIND. USING FLOURED HANDS, GENTLY BRING DOUGH TOGETHER.

PREHEAT OVEN TO 350°F (180°C). WITH FLOURED HANDS, TRANSFER TO LIGHTLY FLOURED SURFACE; DIVIDE IN HALF. ON LARGE BAKING SHEET LINED WITH PARCHMENT, SHAPE DOUGH INTO TWO 9- BY 2-INCH (22 BY 5 CM) RECTANGLES.

BAKE FOR ABOUT 15 MINUTES OR UNTIL LIGHT GOLDEN. REMOVE FROM OVEN AND LET COOL FOR ABOUT 10 MINUTES. TRANSFER TO CUTTING BOARD AND CUT DIAGONALLY INTO 1/2-INCH (1 CM) THICK SLICES. REDUCE OVEN TEMPERATURE TO 300°F (150°C).

STAND SLICES UPRIGHT ON BAKING SHEET AND BAKE FOR ABOUT 20 MINUTES OR UNTIL GOLDEN AND DRY. LET COOL ON RACK. MAKES ABOUT 2$\frac{1}{2}$ DOZEN.

TIP: PLACE IN AIRTIGHT CONTAINER AND FREEZE FOR UP TO 2 MONTHS.

TIP: YOU CAN MAKE SELF-RISING FLOUR USING OUR RECIPE ON PAGE 208.

WHAT KIND OF COOKIES MAKE YOU RICH?
FORTUNE COOKIES!

PEANUT BUTTER CUP COOKIES

CHOCOLATE AND PEANUT BUTTER ARE GREAT
FLAVOR PARTNERS IN THESE FLOURLESS COOKIES.
WE DARE YOU TO JUST STOP AT ONE.

I CUP	CRUNCHY PEANUT BUTTER	250 ML
3/4 CUP	PACKED LIGHT BROWN SUGAR	175 ML
I	LARGE EGG, LIGHTLY BEATEN	I
I TSP	VANILLA	5 ML
3/4 CUP	CHOPPED PEANUT BUTTER CUPS	175 ML

PREHEAT OVEN TO 350°F (180°C). LINE TWO BAKING
SHEETS WITH PARCHMENT PAPER. IN A MEDIUM BOWL,
STIR TOGETHER PEANUT BUTTER, SUGAR, EGG AND
VANILLA UNTIL WELL COMBINED. STIR IN PEANUT BUTTER
CUPS. USING A MINI SCOOP OR A TABLESPOON (15 ML),
DROP DOUGH ONTO PREPARED BAKING SHEETS, SPACING
COOKIES ABOUT 2 INCHES (5 CM) APART.

BAKE, ONE SHEET AT A TIME, FOR 12 MINUTES, UNTIL
COOKIES ARE LIGHTLY BROWNED; COOKIES WILL STILL BE
SOFT AND WILL FIRM UP AS THEY COOL. LET COOL ON
PANS FOR 5 MINUTES, THEN TRANSFER COOKIES TO WIRE
RACKS TO COOL COMPLETELY. MAKES ABOUT 30 COOKIES.

TIP: STORE IN AN AIRTIGHT CONTAINER FOR UP TO 3 DAYS.

TIP: CHOOSE A PEANUT BUTTER THAT HAS A FIRMER
CONSISTENCY, SO THE COOKIES WILL HOLD THEIR
SHAPE BETTER.

OVEN-CARAMELIZED PEARS AND CHOCOLATE

WITH A TOUCH OF DECADENT BITTERSWEET CHOCOLATE, THESE PEARS ARE A DELIGHTFUL FINISH TO ANY MEAL. ENJOY THEM WARM OUT OF THE OVEN WITH A SCOOP OF VANILLA ICE CREAM OR COLD THE NEXT DAY WITH YOGURT FOR BREAKFAST. FOR ADDED CRUNCH, SPRINKLE A FEW TOASTED SLICED ALMONDS ON TOP BEFORE SERVING.

4	RIPE BUT FIRM BARTLETT OR BOSC PEARS (ABOUT 1$\frac{1}{4}$ LBS/625 G)	4
1 CUP	ORANGE JUICE	250 ML
2 TBSP	LIQUID HONEY OR MAPLE SYRUP	30 ML
3 TBSP	GRANULATED SUGAR	45 ML
2 OZ	70% BITTERSWEET CHOCOLATE, CHOPPED	60 G

PREHEAT OVEN TO 400°F (200°C). CUT PEARS IN HALF AND REMOVE CORE. PLACE CUT SIDE DOWN INTO LARGE BAKING DISH.

IN A BOWL, WHISK TOGETHER ORANGE JUICE AND HONEY. POUR OVER PEARS AND COVER WITH FOIL. ROAST FOR 40 MINUTES OR UNTIL PEARS ARE TENDER WHEN PIERCED WITH A KNIFE. UNCOVER AND TURN PEARS OVER. SPRINKLE WITH SUGAR AND BROIL FOR ABOUT 5 MINUTES OR UNTIL CARAMELIZED.

REMOVE FROM OVEN AND SPRINKLE WITH CHOCOLATE; LET STAND FOR 2 MINUTES TO MELT SLIGHTLY. SERVE PEARS WITH SOME OF THE SAUCE. SERVES 8.

BRÛLÉ BANANAS WITH COCONUT AND CINNAMON

THIS SIMPLE DESSERT CAN BE ENJOYED ON ITS OWN OR OVER SOME DELICIOUS VANILLA ICE CREAM — OR YOGURT FOR THOSE FEELING MORE VIRTUOUS. YOU WILL FIND MANY MORE USES FOR THIS SWEET TREAT... WAFFLES OR PANCAKES, ANYONE?

4	LARGE RIPE BUT FIRM BANANAS, CUT IN HALF LENGTHWISE	4
2 TBSP	BUTTER, MELTED	30 ML
$1/2$ CUP	LIGHT BROWN SUGAR	125 ML
$1/2$ TSP	GROUND CINNAMON	2 ML
$1/4$ CUP	FLAKED COCONUT OR SLICED ALMONDS, TOASTED	60 ML

PREHEAT OVEN TO BROIL. PLACE BANANA HALVES ONTO FOIL-LINED BAKING SHEET AND BRUSH WITH BUTTER. IN A SMALL BOWL, PRESS SUGAR THROUGH SIEVE WITH CINNAMON. EVENLY SPREAD ONTO BANANAS.

BROIL FOR ABOUT 3 MINUTES OR UNTIL BUBBLY AND BRÛLÉED. REMOVE FROM OVEN AND, USING A LARGE SPATULA, CAREFULLY SERVE ON DESSERT PLATES SPRINKLED WITH COCONUT. SERVES 4.

TIP: IF YOU HAVE A KITCHEN TORCH, YOU CAN USE THAT TO BRÛLÉ THE BANANAS INSTEAD OF BROILING.

TIP: IF YOU HAVE FOUR OBLONG LARGE RAMEKINS OR SMALL SHALLOW CASSEROLES, PLACE TWO BANANA HALVES IN EACH BEFORE SPRINKLING SUGAR MIXTURE ON. THAT WILL MAKE IT EASIER TO SERVE THIS DESSERT.

BASICS

CHICKEN MEATBALLS

OUR BAKED CHICKEN MEATBALL RECIPE IS EASY AND DELICIOUS. MAKE A BIG BATCH AND FREEZE THEM AND THEY'LL BE READY FOR ANY BUSY DAY MEAL. ENJOY THEM IN OUR CHICKEN MEATBALL FETA WRAPS (PAGE 61) AND CHICKEN MEATBALL VEGGIE SOUP (PAGE 64).

1 LB	LEAN GROUND CHICKEN	500 G
1	LARGE EGG, BEATEN	1
1/4 CUP	SEASONED DRY BREAD CRUMBS	60 ML
1/4 CUP	GRATED PARMESAN CHEESE	60 ML
1/2 TSP	ONION POWDER	2 ML
1/2 TSP	EACH SALT AND BLACK PEPPER	2 ML

PREHEAT OVEN TO 350°F (180°C) AND SET ASIDE A PARCHMENT-LINED BAKING SHEET. IN A BOWL, COMBINE CHICKEN, EGG, BREAD CRUMBS, CHEESE, ONION POWDER, SALT AND PEPPER. USING A MINI ICE CREAM SCOOP OR 2-TBSP (30 ML) MEASURE, ROLL MIXTURE INTO MEATBALLS. PLACE ON PREPARED BAKING SHEET, SPACING THEM APART. BAKE FOR 25 TO 30 MINUTES, UNTIL COOKED THROUGH. MAKES ABOUT 26 MEATBALLS.

TIP: COOKED MEATBALLS CAN BE REFRIGERATED FOR 3 DAYS OR FROZEN FOR UP TO 1 MONTH.

BEEF MEATBALLS

HERE'S A SIMPLE, VERSATILE BAKED BEEF MEATBALL THAT CAN BE ENJOYED IN YOUR FAVORITE PASTA DISH, SANDWICH OR APPETIZER. WE SUGGEST YOU TRY USING THESE IN OUR MEATBALL SUBS (PAGE 62) AND SOUTHWESTERN BEEF MEATBALL SOUP (PAGE 65).

1 LB	LEAN GROUND BEEF	500 G
1/2 CUP	DRY BREAD CRUMBS	125 ML
1	LARGE EGG, BEATEN	1
1	GARLIC CLOVE, MINCED	1
1 TSP	ONION POWDER	5 ML
1/2 TSP	EACH SALT AND BLACK PEPPER	2 ML

IN A LARGE BOWL, MIX BEEF, BREAD CRUMBS, EGG, GARLIC, ONION POWDER, SALT AND PEPPER UNTIL WELL COMBINED. USING A MINI ICE CREAM SCOOP OR 2-TBSP (30 ML) MEASURE, ROLL MIXTURE INTO MEATBALLS. PLACE ON PREPARED BAKING SHEET, SPACING THEM APART. BAKE FOR 25 TO 30 MINUTES, UNTIL COOKED THROUGH. MAKES ABOUT 26 MEATBALLS.

TIP: COOKED MEATBALLS CAN BE REFRIGERATED FOR 3 DAYS OR FROZEN FOR UP TO 1 MONTH.

WHERE DID THE SPAGHETTI AND THE SAUCE GO DANCING? THE MEATBALL!

BASIL PESTO

WHEN YOU HAVE AN ABUNDANCE OF FRESH BASIL AND YOU ARE NOT SURE WHAT TO DO WITH IT, MAKE PESTO! IT'S A GREAT ADDITION TO SALAD DRESSINGS, PASTA OR PIZZA AND MORE. SEE GRILLED HALOUMI CORN SALAD (PAGE 48), HALOUMI-TOPPED SALAD GREENS (PAGE 50), SALSA VERDE FISH TACOS (PAGE 134), MATTHEW'S ROAST SALMON (PAGE 135), SHEET-PAN PROSCIUTTO-WRAPPED SALMON (PAGE 136), BOW TIE SHRIMP AND PESTO PASTA (PAGE 138) AND STEAMED MUSSELS WITH TOMATOES AND SAUSAGE (PAGE 142). IF YOU DON'T USE IT UP IN A FEW DAYS, SIMPLY FREEZE IT FOR A LATER DATE!

2 CUPS	PACKED FRESH BASIL LEAVES	500 ML
3/4 CUP	FRESHLY GRATED PARMESAN CHEESE	175 ML
1/4 CUP	PINE NUTS (OPTIONAL)	60 ML
2	GARLIC CLOVES, MINCED	2
1/2 TSP	SALT	2 ML
PINCH	BLACK PEPPER	PINCH
3/4 CUP	EXTRA VIRGIN OLIVE OIL	175 ML

IN A FOOD PROCESSOR, PULSE TOGETHER BASIL, CHEESE AND PINE NUTS, IF USING, AND GARLIC, SALT AND PEPPER. WITH MACHINE RUNNING, SLOWLY DRIZZLE IN ENOUGH OF THE OIL UNTIL MIXTURE IS SMOOTH. SCRAPE INTO RESEALABLE CONTAINER AND REFRIGERATE FOR UP TO 3 DAYS OR FREEZE FOR UP TO 1 MONTH. MAKES ABOUT 1 CUP (250 ML).

TIP: FOR A MILDER OIL FLAVOR IN YOUR PESTO, SUBSTITUTE CANOLA OIL FOR THE EXTRA VIRGIN OLIVE OIL.

PASTA SAUCE

THIS SAUCE IS THE PERFECT TOMATO PASTA SAUCE TO ENJOY ON ITS OWN FOR PASTA OR IN A RECIPE THAT CALLS FOR A TOMATO BASIL PASTA SAUCE. SEE MEATBALL SUBS (PAGE 62), MADRAS CURRY CHICKEN SOUP (PAGE 66), TOMATO RAVIOLI SOUP (PAGE 67), SPICY SHREDDED BEEF TACOS (PAGE 88), TURKEY GNOCCHI BAKE (PAGE 110) AND HAM AND RICOTTA STUFFED LASAGNA ROLLS (PAGE 116). SIMPLE INGREDIENTS ARE COOKED SLOWLY FOR A DELICIOUS FAMILY FAVORITE.

2	JARS (24 OZ/700 ML EACH) PASSATA (STRAINED TOMATOES)	2
1 CUP	WATER	250 ML
2	SPRIGS FRESH BASIL	2
1	ONION, HALVED	1
3	GARLIC CLOVES, HALVED	3
1/4 CUP	EXTRA VIRGIN OLIVE OIL	60 ML
1 TBSP	DRIED OREGANO LEAVES	15 ML
2 TSP	SALT	10 ML

POUR PASSATA INTO LARGE SAUCEPAN. ADD WATER TO JARS TO RINSE OUT AND ADD TO SAUCEPAN. ADD BASIL, ONION, GARLIC, OIL, OREGANO AND SALT. BRING TO A BOIL; COVER AND REDUCE TO MEDIUM-LOW HEAT. COVER AND COOK FOR ABOUT 2 HOURS OR UNTIL REDUCED SLIGHTLY AND THICKENED.

REMOVE ONION, GARLIC AND BASIL, IF DESIRED; ALTERNATIVELY, PURÉE THEM INTO THE SAUCE. MAKES ABOUT 5 CUPS (1.25 L).

TIP: SAUCE CAN BE MADE UP TO 5 DAYS AHEAD AND REFRIGERATED OR FROZEN FOR UP TO 6 MONTHS.

SELF-RISING FLOUR

SELF-RISING FLOUR IS A HANDY KITCHEN STAPLE
FOR MAKING CAKES, QUICK BREADS AND BISCUITS.
WE USE IT IN OUR RECIPES FOR OLIVE OIL CAKE
(PAGE 189) AND CRANBERRY ORANGE BISCOTTI (PAGE 198.)
THIS FLOUR MIXTURE CAN LOSE ITS EFFECTIVENESS
OVER TIME, SO MAKE IN SMALL BATCHES, LABEL WITH
THE DATE IT WAS MADE AND USE WITHIN ONE YEAR.

I CUP	ALL-PURPOSE FLOUR, MINUS 2 TSP	250 ML
1½ TSP	BAKING POWDER	7 ML
½ TSP	SALT	I ML

IN A BOWL, PLACE FLOUR, BAKING POWDER AND SALT. STIR
TO COMBINE. STORE IN AN AIR-TIGHT CONTAINER.

JUST BURNED 2,000 CALORIES. THAT'S THE LAST TIME
I LEAVE BROWNIES IN THE OVEN WHILE I NAP.

PUMPKIN PIE SPICE MIX

THIS COMBINATION OF WARM SPICES USES INGREDIENTS THAT ARE PROBABLY ALREADY IN YOUR CUPBOARD. USE THIS SPICE MIX IN OUR PUMPKIN SPICE BAKED OATMEAL (PAGE 12) AND PUMPKIN CHEESECAKE BITES (PAGE 190).

3 TBSP	GROUND CINNAMON	45 ML
2 TSP	GROUND GINGER	10 ML
2 TSP	GROUND ALLSPICE	10 ML
1 TSP	GROUND NUTMEG	5 ML
1 TSP	GROUND CLOVES	5 ML

IN A SMALL JAR, MIX ALL INGREDIENTS. COVER TIGHTLY AND STORE IN A COOL, DRY PLACE UP TO 2 MONTHS. MAKES ABOUT $\frac{1}{3}$ CUP (75 ML).

TIP: USE FOR BAKING COOKIES, CUPCAKES, QUICK BREADS AND PIES. YOU CAN EVEN ADD A SPRINKLE TO YOUR COFFEE AS IT'S BREWING.

LETTUCE CELEBRATE!

Library and Archives Canada Cataloguing in Publication

Title: Best of Bridge 5-ingredient cooking : 125 recipes for fast & easy meals.
Other titles: Best of Bridge five-ingredient cooking | 5-ingredient cooking | Five-ingredient cooking
Names: Richards, Emily, author. | Kong, Sylvia, author.
Description: Written by Emily Richards and Sylvia Kong.
Identifiers: Canadiana 20200269682 | ISBN 9780778806776 (hardcover)
Subjects: LCSH: Quick and easy cooking. | LCGFT: Cookbooks.
Classification: LCC TX833.5 .R53 2020 | DDC 641.5/55—dc23

ICE HOCKEY IS BASICALLY PEOPLE WEARING KNIFE SHOES FIGHTING EACH OTHER WITH LONG STICKS FOR THE LAST OREO COOKIE.

INDEX

olives
  Chicken Tapenade Puff Rolls, 106
  Pizza Perogy Bake, 122
  Skillet Beef Fast-Fry Steaks with
    Tomatoes and Olives, 85
onions
  Fig Jam and Goat Cheese Tart, 30
  Firecracker Noodles, 162
  Pizza Soup, 74
  Potato, Bean and Tomato Salad, 52
  Simple Split Pea Soup, 71
  Skillet Beef Fast-Fry Steaks with
    Tomatoes and Olives, 85
orange
  Cranberry Orange Biscotti, 198
  Orange Wheatberry Apple Salad,
    46
  Oven-Caramelized Pears and
    Chocolate, 201

P

pasta and noodles. *See also* gnocchi
  Bow Tie Shrimp and Pesto Pasta,
    138
  Chunky Chicken Minestrone, 69
  Egg and Pasta Frittata, 170
  Firecracker Noodles, 162
  Ham and Ricotta Stuffed Lasagna
    Rolls, 116
  Prosciutto and Pea Pasta Bake, 123
  Ravioli in Balsamic Cream, 169
  Spaghetti al Limone, 157
  Tomato Ravioli Soup, 67
Pasta Sauce, 207
pastry (puff and phyllo). *See also* tart
    shells
  Chicken Tapenade Puff Rolls, 106
  Goat Cheese and Pear Bites, 38

Rustic Open-Face Berry Tart, 186
  Sausage Turnovers, 120
Paul's Favorite Soy Sauce Chicken,
    103
peanut butter. *See also* satay sauce
  Grilled Peanut Butter Pineapple
    Chicken Skewers, 104
  Peanut Butter Cup Cookies, 200
  Thai Chicken Salad, 55
peas. *See also* chickpeas
  Prosciutto and Pea Pasta Bake, 123
  Simple Split Pea Soup, 71
Pecan Turkey Cutlets, 109
peppers
  Egg and Pasta Frittata, 170
  Egg Pizza (variation), 14
  Grilled Mussels with Mango
    Chutney, 148
  Hummus Feta Pepper Pizza, 155
  Pimento Cheese, 24
  Potato, Bean and Tomato Salad (tip),
    52
  Roasted Corn and Bacon Salad, 53
  Roasted Red Pepper Cashew Pasta
    Sauce, 161
  Sausage-Stuffed Jalapeño Peppers,
    James's, 28
  Sheet-Pan Prosciutto-Wrapped
    Salmon, 136
pesto (as ingredient), 206
  Bow Tie Shrimp and Pesto Pasta,
    138
  Chicken Tapenade Puff Rolls, 106
  Grilled Haloumi Corn Salad, 48
  Haloumi-Topped Salad Greens, 50
  Roasted Red Pepper Cashew Pasta
    Sauce, 161
  Roast Salmon, Matthew's, 135
  Salsa Verde Fish Tacos, 134

T

Tahini Honey Chicken, 102

tart shells
  Brown Sugar Berry Tarts, 196
  Goat Cheese and Compote Tart, 39

Thai Chicken Salad, 55

Thai Coconut Chickpeas, 160

tofu
  Firecracker Noodles, 162
  Miso Tofu and Vegetables, 158

tomatoes. *See also specific types (below)*; tomato sauces
  Ale-Braised Lamb, 128
  BAT Salad, 51
  Chilled Tomato Soup, 72
  Chunky Chicken Minestrone, 69
  Garlic Tomato Seafood Risotto, 146
  Grilled Flank Steak with Bruschetta Topping, 76
  Grilled Haloumi Corn Salad, 48
  Pasta Sauce, 207
  Potato, Bean and Tomato Salad, 52
  Steamed Mussels with Tomatoes and Sausage, 142

tomatoes, grape
  Bow Tie Shrimp and Pesto Pasta, 138
  Crab Avocado Salad, 54
  Haloumi-Topped Salad Greens, 50
  Lentil Bowl, 156
  Pizza Perogy Bake, 122
  Roasted Eggplant Tomato Dip, 43
  Skillet Beef Fast-Fry Steaks with Tomatoes and Olives, 85

tomatoes, sun-dried
  Chicken Meatball Feta Wraps, 61
  Eggplant Tacos, 32
  Sun-Dried Tomato and Artichoke Dip, 44
  Thai Chicken Salad, 55

tomato sauces. *See also* salsa
  Egg Pizza, 14
  Ham and Ricotta Stuffed Lasagna Rolls, 116
  Madras Curry Chicken Soup, 66
  Meatball Subs, 62
  Pizza Soup, 74
  Pulled Pork Pizza Braid, 124
  Spicy Shredded Beef Tacos, 88
  Superfast Egg and Ricotta Lasagna, 172
  Tomato Ravioli Soup, 67
  Turkey Gnocchi Bake, 110

tortillas and tortilla chips
  Quinoa Breakfast Burritos, 18
  Salsa Chicken, 97
  Salsa Verde Fish Tacos, 134
  Spicy Shredded Beef Tacos, 88

turkey. *See also* chicken
  Pecan Turkey Cutlets, 109
  Quinoa Breakfast Burritos, 18
  Scrambled Egg Naans, 16
  Turkey Gnocchi Bake, 110

V

veal. *See* beef

vegetables. *See also* greens; *specific vegetables*
  Beef and Black Bean Stir-Fry, 80
  Chicken Meatball Veggie Soup, 64
  Chunky Chicken Minestrone, 69
  Cranberry Bacon Brussels Sprouts, 176

IT ALL ENDS WITH BISCUITS AND WINE.
—ITALIAN PROVERB